PIECING WITH PIXELS

UNIQUE QUILTS
FROM YOUR OWN IMAGES

Sandra Hart & Gudny Campbell

American Quilter's Society

P. O. Box 3290 • Paducah, KY 42002-3290
www.AmericanQuilter.com

Located in Paducah, Kentucky, the American Quilter's Society (AQS) is dedicated to promoting the accomplishments of today's quilters. Through its publications and events, AQS strives to honor today's quiltmakers and their work and to inspire future creativity and innovation in quiltmaking.

© 2009, Authors, Sandra Hart and Gudny Campbell

EXECUTIVE EDITOR: ANDI MILAM REYNOLDS
GRAPHIC DESIGN: MARTY TURNER
COVER DESIGN: MICHAEL BUCKINGHAM
PHOTOGRAPHY: CHARLES R. LYNCH

American Quilter's Society
P. O. Box 3290 • Paducah, KY 42002-3290
www.AmericanQuilter.com

Additional copies of this book may be ordered from the American Quilter's Society, PO Box 3290, Paducah, KY 42002-3290, or online at www.AmericanQuilter.com.

Library of Congress Cataloging-in-Publication Data

Hart, Sandra G. (Sandra Gail)
  Piecing with pixels : unique quilts from your own images / by Sandra Hart and Gudny Campbell.
    p. cm.
  Includes index.
  ISBN 978-1-57432-968-1
  1. Quilting. 2. Adobe Photoshop. 3. Photography--Digital techniques. I. Campbell, Gudny. II. Title.

TT835.H342 2009
746.46--dc22

2008047406

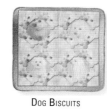

BUBBLES

DOG BISCUITS

MOONLIT LEAVES

COASTAL PATH

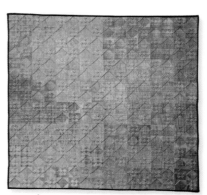

SQUARE COOKIES

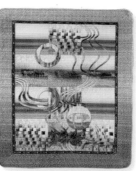

OCEAN ROAD

AUTUMN LEAVES

CHECKERBOARD

CALIFORNIA BEAUTY

Piecing with Pixels shows you how to transform your favorite photos into beautiful and unique quilts using Adobe® Photoshop® Elements tools. You will learn how to digitally piece, appliqué, and embellish shapes cut with Photoshop Elements Cookie Cutters to create the project quilts and print them on fabric. Our designs are based on one or more of the 568 shapes from the Cookie Cutter menu and "fabric" we created with a variety of Photoshop Elements tools.

Going far beyond simply transferring photos to fabric, we will share what we have discovered about how to create a dazzling Digital Stash starting with any image you can photograph, scan, or download and then transforming it with Photoshop Elements filters. Think of the results as "fat quarters" that you can save, further modify, and reuse over and over.

Pieces of a Digital Stash are created from photos.

A whole new world of creative options will unfold as you learn how to create unique and personally meaningful quilts that represent a memorable trip, event, person, place, or accomplishment. Alternatively, you may create an entirely abstract work of art filled with gorgeous colors and textures. The possibilities for one-of-a-kind fiber art are endless.

Even better, one of the many benefits of digital "piecing" and "appliqué" is that completed quilt blocks aren't used up when they are used; they can be reprinted, resized, recolored, or transformed with embellishments over and over again. Multiple blocks can be combined to create sampler quilts, table runners, pillows, clothing, greeting cards, or scrapbook pages.

Chapter 1, Getting Started, summarizes computer and printer requirements; Photoshop Elements software versions; acquiring digital images from cameras, scanners, and the Internet; and image resolution.

Chapter 2, Digital Piecing & Applique, shows you how to use Photoshop Elements to (1) Create the component shapes for a block from a solid color, photograph, or Digital Stash. This step is analogous to cutting fabric in preparation for piecing or appliqué using scissors or a rotary cutter. (2) Combine these shapes with a background. This step is analogous to sewing pieces of fabric together with needle and thread or a sewing machine. (3) Refine the process to produce the exact result you have in mind (e.g., rotating, resizing, flipping, or ordering shapes). These steps are analogous to fussy-cutting to ensure that each piece is cut from the most appropriate part of a patterned fabric.

Chapter 3, Creating & Embellishing "Fabric," illustrates how to create a Digital Stash with Photoshop Elements filters and change the visual appearance of a block by "frosting" it with layer styles or playing with color. This chapter covers topics that are somewhat analogous to embellishing or highlighting a quilt block created with commercial fabric, needle, and thread.

Chapter 4, Designing & Printing, describes how to audition and combine blocks on a digital "design wall" and add a digital border. The Printing on Fabric section explains how to prepare fabric for and print on personal ink-jet printers as well as wide-format commercial printers.

Cookie Cutter shapes cut from solid color, flower photo, and Digital Stash "embellished" with bevels and shadows

Chapter 5, Projects, includes step-by-step instructions for nine projects that range in complexity from multiple copies of a simple block created with one Cookie Cutter shape, to traditional quilt blocks and innovative designs composed of multiple blocks and layers of shapes.

Chapter 6, Pixel Versatility, provides suggestions for resizing, reusing, or recycling your creations.

We suggest you read chapters 1 through 4 before starting the projects.

Example of one digitally "pieced" and one "appliquéd" block

ABOUT THE AUTHORS

With over 50 combined years of quilting and computing experience, we have recently become enthusiastic pioneers in digital quilting through exploration of widely available hardware and software. Our quilts range from a mix of our digitally designed and printed fabric with commercial fabric to those entirely developed on a computer and printed as a completed top. To create these quilts, we use different types of computers (Sandy has a Mac, Gudny a PC) and different versions of Adobe® Photoshop® Elements software in combination with different aspects of the quilting traditions of piecing and appliqué. Our quilts have been shown at Houston International Quilt Festival and seen in quilting books and magazines.

We started collaborating in 2006, co-teaching several 2- and 5-day workshops on "Technology Is a Quilter's Best Friend" and co-wrote the article "Digital Delights: Appliqué and Piecing by Computer" published in the January 2008 issue of American Quilter.

Sandra Hart has been teaching people how to print images onto fabric and incorporate these images into quilts since 1996. Most of her teaching experience

was gained in California and Oregon quilt shops where she offered classes that lasted from several hours to several days. Her traditional and computer-assisted quilts have been shown in numerous quilt shows and appeared in Photo Fun, edited by Cyndy Lyle Rymer, and Innovative Fabric Imagery for Quilts by Cindy Lyle Rymer and Lynn Koolish. She is a Macintosh® computer expert and has been using Microsoft® PowerPoint and Adobe® Photoshop® software to create quilts since the mid-1990s. Sandy worked as a NASA scientist until her retirement in 2007.

Gudny Campbell has been teaching people how to use computers since 1984, and has taught adults and children how to apply innovative techniques, such as digital design and fabric painting, to add interest to their quilts. Her quilts were included in the books Innovative Fabric Imagery for Quilts by Cyndy Lyle Rymer and Lynn Koolish and Circle Play: Simple Designs for Fabulous Fabrics by Reynola Pakusich.

Gudny worked for the Navy as a computer specialist until she retired in 2003, managing an intranet network and microcomputers for 300 users.

Their website is **www. CreatingWithPixels. com.**

Sandra Hart   **Gudny Campbell**

As you will see, we start many of the projects with one or more images. Then, we start playing with them using Photoshop Elements filters and other enhancements to create gorgeous textures and colors — our fabric. Then, Cookie Cutters make short work of the "piecing" and "appliqué" steps. Finally, we add layer styles to create dimensional edges and fine-tune the colors to get just the effect we imagined. Our digital photos are like tubes of paint and the Photoshop Elements workspace a palette where we combine and transform them into one-of-a-kind works of art using a variety of tools.

Where do we get these images? We take hundreds of snapshots of scenery, natural and man-made objects, and close-ups of interesting textures with our digital cameras. In addition, Sandy downloads images from Internet sites where people share their photographs or she purchases CDs filled with images of the type needed for a particular quilt. While this is a wonderful source of stash-building images, be sure you have permission from the owner of the image before you download and use them.

Nearly any image can serve as the springboard for making digital "fabric" although interesting textures are the crucial feature. These pages show a few of our photos that have proven to be really good starting points for quilts or particularly successful Digital Stash pieces. Gudny usually makes her digital fabrics as she creates a specific quilt.

Some of Gudny's favorite stash-building photos

Most of her quilts have started with pictures from nature — clouds, bark, flowers, and leaves. Sandy creates stash in her spare time and saves it for future use. When she makes a quilt, she opens dozens of files that originated from many different photos. She has been a little more eclectic in her choices of stash-inspiring images: lots of flowers, leaves and bark, rocks and dirt, copper roofs, balloons, fire, clouds, sunrises and sunsets, food, beaches, fish, toys, knitting, paintings, and even a gravestone. Either approach works, so be creative!

SOFTWARE

You can obtain excellent results with Photoshop Elements v4.0 through v7.0. While there are some differences among these versions, they are generally insignificant and we will try to point them out as we describe how to make quilts with Photoshop Elements. As new software updates become available, check with Adobe Technical Support for changes to menu or main screens. Before upgrading or buying, download a free 30-day trial of the current Photoshop Elements version from the Adobe Web site and try it. Similarly, while there are some differences between the Mac and PC versions of Photoshop Elements, they are insignificant compared to the similarities.

HARDWARE

Your computer and printer will become basic quilting tools, just like your sewing machine, rotary cutter, and iron. The decision about what type of computer to buy is very personal and it's likely you will start with whatever you already own or can borrow. You can create wonderful results with almost any computer; Sandy uses a three-year-old Mac while Gudny uses a new PC. This said, however, plenty of computer memory and speed are a big benefit when processing and saving a lot of images. A digital quilt saved as a PSD file can consume as much as 250 mBytes of memory, and the storage space for all those pieces of Digital Stash adds up. Gudny got speed by purchasing a new computer with two GB of memory and more disk space by adding a removable drive, while Sandy added more memory to her existing computer and makes do with the memory she has by saving most creations in formats that require less memory.

We both use portable computers and have gotten used to making large images on small displays. However, additional display space would be helpful. Gudny uses a mouse with a scroll that makes zooming in and out a breeze. She points and clicks her way to beautiful quilt tops. Sandy uses the touch pad on her Mac and relies on keyboard shortcuts as much as possible.

DIGITIZING IMAGES

Because the images you use in your quilts may come from a variety of sources, it may be necessary to adjust their size and resolution so they will be compatible. If the image you would like to use is not in digital form there are several choices — photograph it with a digital camera and import it directly into your computer, photograph it with a film camera and ask for a photo CD instead of prints when you get your film developed, or scan it.

Resolution

Image resolution is expressed as the number of pixels per inch (ppi). Although you can increase the size of any digital image to any size, the "spaces" between the original pixels may become so noticeable that the printed version may look awful. Photoshop Elements will do its best to fill them, but you may not be happy with the results.

Computer-screen resolution is generally 72–96 ppi. However, higher resolutions of at least 240–300 ppi are generally required when printing on paper. Thus, a 72 ppi image from your cell phone or the Internet that looks fine on your screen may not print well. Because the fabric you will be printing on has a grain (described in terms of threads per inch), resolutions as low as 150–240 ppi may be sufficient to look good when printed. Images saved in JPEG format with at least "good" quality are sufficient for nearly everything you will want to do. The TIFF format offers higher resolution, but at the cost of huge file sizes.

The crucial point is to stick with a size and resolution for all of the images you use in one project. All sorts of unexpected (and annoying) consequences will result when you mix images with different resolutions. "Cookies" cut from images that are too small will end up looking as though they have a bite taken out of them! The lesson here is to always check the size and resolution of any image before you start adding filters or cutting cookies!

Scanners

When choosing a scanner, faster is always better. Be sure to check it for compatibility with your com-

puter. Other than that, one is probably as good as another for this purpose; all scanners offer adequate resolution for this task. Most scanners come with Mac and PC drivers as well as software to make scanning and editing easy. Even inexpensive scanners will work seamlessly with image editing software, such as Photoshop Elements, as long as they are a similar vintage as the computer.

Cameras

Digital cameras are a wonderful way to obtain lots of images to incorporate into your masterpieces. As long as the pictures taken on the "best" setting are approximately the same size that you will be printing (with a resolution of at least 240 ppi) you should have no problems.

The advantage of digital pictures over scanning is flexibility — you aren't limited to what will fit on the bed of your scanner. And, it can take as little as 10 minutes from idea to execution and printing on fabric!

Many cell phones include a camera, offering another option, but the resolution of the results may not be adequate. It is possible to capture the same images with a film camera, but you have to wait until the film is processed and saved in digital form on a CD. As with scanners, most digital cameras offer software that makes it easy to download images and perform basic editing.

Some of Sandy's favorite stash-building photos

THE BASICS

The following describes and demonstrates some of the basic skills you will need to start using Adobe® Photoshop® Elements. Please consult Photoshop Elements Help for more complete information about how to use this program. In later sections, we describe additional skills you will need to create project quilts, such as rotating, coloring, layering, or "frosting" shapes created with the Cookie Cutter tool. When following the steps to create one of the project quilts, you may want to refer back to these "how to" sections.

Think of this first section as learning how to create basic sugar cookie dough that will serve as the foundation for additional ingredients, layers, frosting, and fancy decorations. Although we usually create quilts using our images or Digital Stash to fill and digitally "appliqué" or "piece" blocks, Photoshop Elements provides a number of options in the basic menus that we will explore first. We wrote the instructions for the PC version of Photoshop Elements

(v4.0 through 7.0). Mac users (v4.0, 6.0) need to think "Apple/Command" when the instructions say "Control" and "Option" when the instructions say "Alt." You can achieve similar results with Adobe® Photoshop® Creative Suite® software, but the process is different and more difficult; there is no Cookie Cutter. Custom Shape Menu offers the same shapes, but they are applied using a different sequence of steps that we don't cover in *Piecing with Pixels*.

In most cases, there is more than one way to create the blocks and quilts in this book using different Photoshop Elements tools. These options are analogous to the choices quilters routinely make between scissors and rotary cutters (to cut fabric patches) or between hand and machine (to piece, appliqué, and quilt). Try different methods to see which working style suits you. Sequences of selections made using the mouse to click on options in tool bars, palette bins, or pull-down menus are surrounded by brackets [ ] and separated by > to indicate order. Keyboard shortcuts are surrounded by < >. When keyboard shortcuts consist of more than one selection, press everything at the same time.

Customize Photoshop Elements

Set up Photoshop Elements the way we do:
1. Launch Photoshop Elements and open the editor.
2. Create a new blank file.
3. Click on the following options from the pull-down menu and a check will appear in front of the option.

- **Images**
Be sure you work in the "Tile" or "Cascade" mode, particularly if you want to drag images from one file to another. The Tile mode allows you to freely display, position, and size multiple files on your display at the same time. [Window>Images>Tile or Cascade mode]

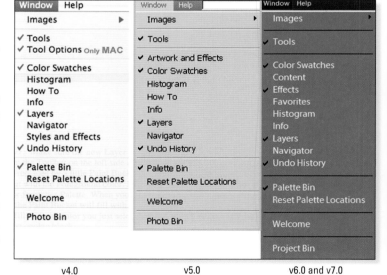

v4.0   v5.0   v6.0 and v7.0

Hint

If you suddenly can't work back and forth between multiple files, check if Images has reverted accidentally to its default (Maximize mode). Change back to Tile or Cascade mode and all will be well.

- **Preferences**
On a PC, select [Edit> Preferences>General menu]. On a Mac v4.0, select [Photoshop Elements>Preferences>General menu]. Then check:
✓ Save Palette locations
✓ Set Show Tool Tips
✓ Zoom with Scroll Wheel (If you have a mouse with a center scroll wheel you can use the wheel to zoom an image in or out.)

- **Color Setup**
Under Edit>Color Setup ("Color Settings" in v. 6)
✓ Always Optimize for Printing

Set up Grid dimensions.

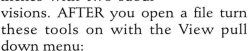

• Ruler, Grid, Snap To Grid

Displaying a ruler and grid in the workspace makes it easy to position multiple objects. Set up a grid by selecting [Edit>Preferences>Grid] for PC users or [Photoshop Elements>Preferences >Grid] for Mac users. In the example, we specified gridlines every 4 inches with two subdivisions. AFTER you open a file turn these tools on with the View pull down menu:

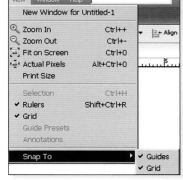

View pull-down menu (turn on Rulers, Grid, Snap To Grid)

✓ Rulers
✓ Grid (when positioning shapes)
✓ Snap To Grid (when positioning shapes)

Create the block background

1. Open a new file.

To create a blank work area, open a new blank file by selecting the following from pull-down menus using the mouse [File>New>Blank File] or pressing <CTRL n>. Name the file. For many of the projects, we will ask you to create a work area with these characteristics:

– *Width:* 8 inches
– *Height:* 8 inches
– *Resolution:* 240 pixels/inch (ppi)
– *Color Mode:* RGB color
– *Contents:* White or Transparent

Gudny prefers "transparent" — it produces a new file with a bottom layer that can be used like any other layer. Sandy prefers White or Background Color — it produces a locked background that provides a solid-colored work area beneath subsequent layers.

2. Open an existing file.

If you want to start with a photo or Digital Stash file instead of a blank file, open it by selecting [File>Open] or pressing <CTRL o>. Select "Files of type: All Formats" when browsing to find the file(s) to open on your computer, CD, or removable memory. Always check the dimensions of each file as you open it to be sure it is appropriate for the next steps. If it isn't, change its dimensions and/ or resolution using the Crop tool <c> or the Resize [Image>Size>Resize] or press <CTRL ALT i>. Refer to Resize, Rotate, and Flip on pages 16–18 for details.

3. Change a Photoshop Elements background to a regular layer.

It is usually best to work with a regular layer rather than a locked Background layer; the background is a special type of layer that exists when you open a JPEG image file or a new blank file with a non-transparent background. Because there are some limitations with what you can do with the background, you can convert it to a regular layer by double clicking on it in the Layers palette (PC users) or select [Layer>New>Layer from Background] (Mac users). (See page 18.) Its name will change to Layer 0. You could also just add a new layer to work on by pressing <SHIFT CTRL n> or duplicate it <CTRL j>.

Layers

The Layers palette contains selectable icons and information about each layer: a little eye, a thumbnail image of its content, and its name. Clicking on the eye makes the layer visible (or not). Double- or right-clicking on the name allows you to rename it anything you wish.

1. Create a new layer.

There are several ways to create a new, blank layer. The easiest is clicking on the "Create a New Layer" icon (see page 19) at the top left corner of the Layers palette or pressing <SHIFT CTRL n>.

As you create additional layers, you will notice in the workspace that images in upper layers can hide images in lower layers unless some or all of the images in the upper layer are smaller or somewhat transparent (notice the opacity slider above the Layers palette). It is easy to change the order of the layers by positioning your cursor in the name area of the layer box until the "Hand" symbol appears. Nudge any layers (except the background) up or down the stack with your mouse until they are in the order you need. Look for more information in the More About Layers section, pages 18–21.

2. Duplicate a layer.

You can also create a new layer by making a copy of an existing layer. For example, if you open a photo and work in that file you might want to duplicate it and work on that layer rather than the original. There are many ways to duplicate layers including:

– *Use the layers pull-down menu* at the top of the screen. [LAYER>DUPLICATE]

– *Select the layer to be copied,* be sure it is visible, and press <CTRL j>.

– *Cntrl click (Mac) or right click (PC)* on a layer in the Layers palette and select Duplicate Layer.

– *Drag a layer from another file* into the current workspace (this will be covered in more detail later).

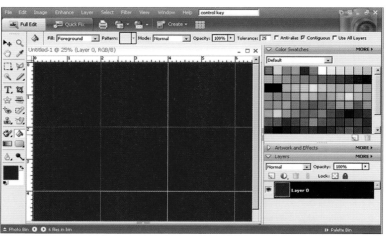

Color Swatches Palette and 1-layer workspace

3. Move the contents of a layer or entire file to another.

It is easy to move objects (on layers by themselves) from one file to another with your mouse. Be sure that both the original and destination files are open and visible on the desktop. Click on the layer (or drag the Marquee tool around a specific area of the layer) with the Move tool <v> active. With the mouse button held down, move the mouse across the desktop from the workspace of the original file into the middle of the destination file workspace. When you release the button, a copy of the selected image will appear in the destination file in a new layer. Alternatively, you can click on the NAME of the layer you wish to move in the Layers palette of the original file, and drag it into the destination file as above.

4. Color a blank layer.

Click on the Paint Bucket tool in the toolbar on the left side of the Photoshop Elements workspace with your mouse or press <k>. The cursor will be replaced by a little Paint Bucket icon. If you touch its tip anywhere on a Background layer it will fill with the foreground color. To change the Foreground color, click on one of the color chips in the Color Swatches palette and the Paint Bucket will fill with that color. Now, when you use the Paint Bucket, the layer (or whatever object you selected) will fill with that color. Try creating a new layer and filling it with a different color and look for more information in the Color Play section, pages 31–35.

Cutting a cookie shape

Photoshop Elements offers 583 shapes that you can cut from any layer using the Cookie Cutter tool. These shapes are vector graphics that can be scaled to any size and resolution without losing detail or clarity. The cookie cutter doesn't care what the layer contains: a solid color, layer style, photograph, Digital Stash, or any other image you can imagine. Think of a set of cookie cutters that can cut shapes from any rolled dough—sugar cookie, chocolate, or gingerbread. The magic comes from the way you combine the cut shapes with embellishments and other layers filled with different colors, textures, or images. The following will get you started (later sections will elaborate):

1. Select the layer you plan to use.

This may be the "Background" if you open a photo or Digital Stash file. Be sure it is visible and at the top of the stack if there are multiple layers. If this layer is a duplicate of the previous layer, click on the eye next to the bottom layer so it will be invisible. This will allow you to see the shape after it has been cut.

2. Select the Cookie Cutter tool in the toolbar.

Click on its symbol (heart in v4.0, star in v5.0, v6.0, and v7.0) or press <q>.

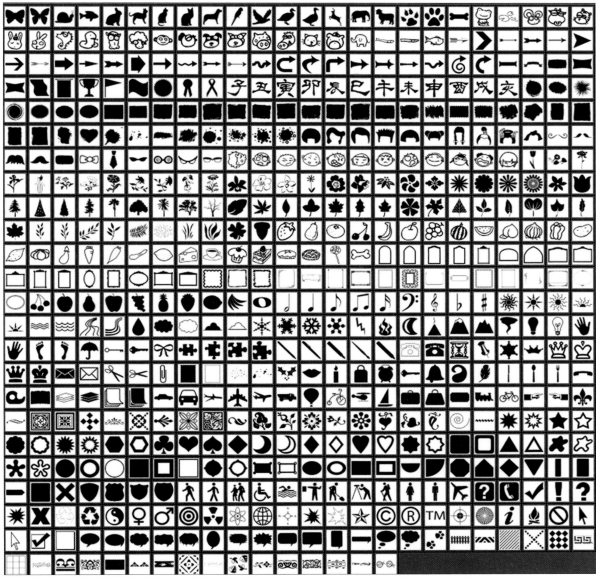

Photoshop Elements Cookie Cutter Shapes

3. Select a shape.

Use the Shape pull-down menu in the Cookie Cutter Options bar above the workspace. Click on the little arrow on the right at the top of the menu to display a specific submenu or "All Photoshop Elements Shapes." Scroll down to see all of the shapes shown, try displaying the Ornaments submenu, and select Leaf Ornament 1. This is an example of a stencil shape.

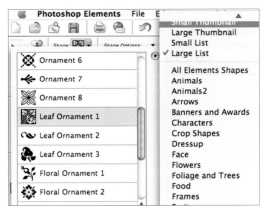

Selecting a Cookie Cutter Shape from a shapes submenu

4. Select Cookie Cutter Options.

– *Shape Options:* The Shape Options pull-down menu allows you to specify the proportions and size of the cookie cutter. Start with Defined Proportions. Later, try Fixed Size (enter a specific width and height in inches) and "Unconstrained" to see how they work. If the shape you cut turns out to be the wrong size, it can always be changed later (see Resize, Rotate & Flip on pages 16–18).

– *Feather:* Feathering softens a cookie's hard edges, blurring them and blending them into the background. While it produces lovely effects and Sandy has used it in several quilts, we didn't use it in any of the book projects.

– *Crop:* If on, the entire file will end up the exact dimensions of the cookie shape after it is cut. Crop should be **off** when you are cutting a cookie shape and you do **not** want to change the dimensions of the entire workspace. Crop should be **on** when you cut a cookie shape out of a larger image and then drag the result into a block file.

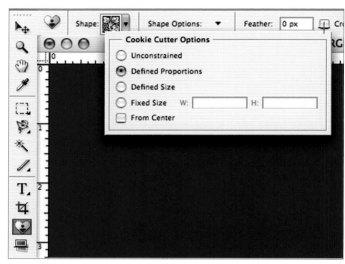

Setting up Cookie Cutter Options from the Options pull-down menu

5. Position Cookie Cutters.

When you click on the work area again, a small PLUS sign appears, and the drop-down menu disappears. Hold the mouse down and drag it to the desired size. (If you select Fixed Size, Photoshop Elements will automatically position a cookie cutter of the selected size over the photo, Digital Stash, or painted layer.) Move the cookie cutter around with the mouse until it is completely within the workspace. Once you have begun to position and size the cookie cutter, the Free Transform Options bar replaces the Cookie Cutter Options bar.

Free Transform Options bar

6. Fussy Cut.

The digital equivalent of this technique is possible with Photoshop Elements. When the cookie cutter is smaller than the layer to which it will be applied, you can select the part of the image from which the "cookie" is cut, much like moving an acrylic template over patterned fabric. You can also move part of the Cookie Cutter beyond the boundaries of the workspace to cut just part of a shape. This trick will be used in both AUTUMN LEAVES and CALIFORNIA BEAUTY projects. Try some or all of the following:

– *Center it:* Slide the template around until it is centered over the best part of a patterned layer.

– *Free Rotate it:* Rotate the template by moving the cursor just outside its image in the workspace and dragging it around.

– *Flip it:* To cut the mirror image of a template, grab one side of the bounding box, drag it across the template to the other side and keep going until the template is reoriented. Then, reposition the cursor in the middle of the template and reposition it, if necessary.

– *Reorient it:* To rotate the cookie cutter by a specific amount, enter a value in the Free Transform Options bar. Values from 0° to 180° will rotate the cookie cutter clockwise. Values from –1° to –179° will rotate it counterclockwise. This technique will be used in the DOG BISCUIT and COASTAL PATH projects.

7. Cut it.
Click on the green OK area [✓] (v5.0, v6.0, and v7.0) or press <ENTER> to cut the selected shape. To start again, click on Cancel (v5.0, v6.0, and v7.0) or press <ESC> (v4.0). We will refer to the results as a "cookie" or an appliqué. Try Project 1 (MOONLIT LEAVES) to make a quilt with your new skills.

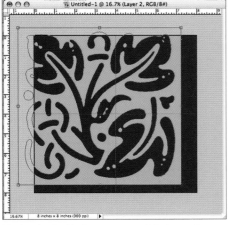

Moving the Cookie Cutter to center it in the workspace

Free Rotating a cookie shape

Your first cookie!

Undo!

Photoshop Elements is infinitely forgiving; you can always get back to a point when you still liked your creation if you make a mistake or are unhappy with your choices. Back up by following these steps:

   1. Click on the Undo Arrow (Photoshop Elements v4.0, v6.0, and v7.0)

   2. Select [Edit>Undo].

   3. Press <CTRL z>.

   4. Move up one or more steps in the Undo History palette.

Save the Image

1. Use the PSD format.

You can stop here and save the shape by entering [File>Save] or pressing <CTRL s>. This graphics file format will preserve the layers and transparency, but takes more disk space. Transparency is important because it allows you to move a saved appliqué shape from one file to another without having to delete its background first.

2. Use the JPEG format.

This format requires less disk space but reduces future options; you can no longer access multiple layers if you reopen the image. Photoshop Elements automatically flattens the image when you select JPEG from the Format pull-down menu that appears in the Save As box. [File>Save as] or <CTRL SHIFT s>. Provide a new name and destination folder, click SAVE, then specify Image Quality (we usually choose something between 9/High/Large file and 12/Maximum). If you save a cookie shape that has a transparent background as a JPEG, the background loses its transparency and becomes white. This background will have to be selected and deleted (using the Magic Wand) before you can use the shape in the future. Also, JPEG files lose quality every time they are opened, edited, and saved, so make a habit of using "Save As" instead of "Save."

3. Use the PNG format.

This useful format preserves all of the information, including transparency, but takes less space than a PSD format.

MORE ABOUT PHOTOS

Liberate your digital photos and be creative! The blocks and quilts you create will be uniquely yours, because the photographs you use will be your own. The next example shows a block and digital quilt created entirely from two photos, a red rose background and light rose cookie shape.

Block and quilt example created from two photos

Opening and closing photos

Always check the image size and resolution [Image>Resize>Image Size] and make sure it is the same in all the files you use for a project. You can also use the Crop tool to resize if you set size and resolution in the Crop Options bar; this is very handy when you want to resize multiple files.

When you save a photo, always Save As. You want to preserve your original to work with another time.

Touching up photos

If you think your photo needs a quick touchup, click on Quick Fix or (v6.0 click on Quick) on the top bar.

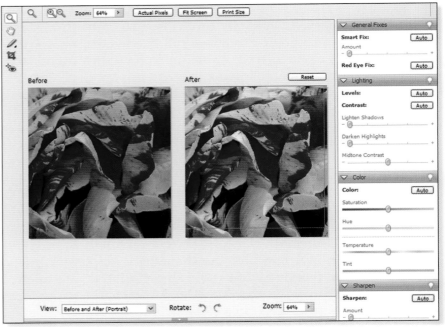

QuickFix Screen

Try Smart Fix first. Play around with the other options. Return to Standard Edit or Full Edit when you are happy with the result, or click reset to revert to your original image before leaving Quick Fix.

You can also select the lighting, color, and sharpen options individually via the Enhance menu.

Hint

Resources lists some recommended books and Web sites.

Fussy cutting

Fussy cutting via the Crop tool <c> or when creating a cookie shape allows you to focus on an area. Your photo must be larger than the area you want to fussy cut. Note the crop options bar on top.

When creating the block on the previous page, only the center of the red rose was used for the background; the black was cropped away.

When you cut a cookie shape, if you want a specific part of the photo to appear, select the Defined Size option, and then free rotate by moving the mouse around outside the bounding box and/or resize by dragging the mouse on the bounding box.

Crop fussy-cutting example

Scaling photos

The following example shows how to use the Crop tool <c>, to get a group of photos so they are the right scale and aspect ratio before cutting cookies and incorporating them into a traditional block like Drunkard's Path, which is similar to project 2.

Cookie fussy-cutting example

Original photos   Cropped photos   Cookie shapes

Drunkard's Path block

Other ideas

You could create a quilt using all the cookie frames, alternating photo and solid squares, or creating "I Spy" hexagon photo shapes. Many of the projects or their variations use realistic photos and mix them with Digital Stash or Frosting.

"I Spy" hexagon photo shapes

Alternating photo and solid color squares

"Rogues Gallery" by Sandy Hart created using old photos and cookie frame shapes

RESIZE, ROTATE & FLIP

At different points in the process of creating pieced and appliqué blocks, you will need to change the dimensions or orientation of one layer or the entire multi-layered image. Below are the basics; there will be more in later sections as well.

Cropping when cutting a shape

The simplest way to create a cookie and create a new file that is the size you specified and fills the workspace is to use the Crop option in the Cookie Cutter Options bar before you start. The advantages are: (1) You can easily modify the size of the result further using commands listed below; and (2) If you drag it into another file, no extraneous parts of the original (that are not visible, given the size of the current workspace) may come along as well. Be warned, however, that this selection will also crop every other layer in that file as well. If you want to retain the dimensions of the original file when cutting a shape, be sure the Crop option in the Cookie Cutter toolbar is "off."

Resize a file

1. Change the image size.

In the development of any image from a single layer to a multi-layered masterpiece, you can change the size and/or aspect ratio of the entire workspace (and thus the contents of all layers) by selecting [Image>Resize>Image Size] or pressing <CTRL ALT i>. The options you choose depend on what you are trying to accomplish. To maintain the original aspect ratio, check Constrain Proportions and enter either a new height or width; any change made to one dimension will also affect the other so the image is not distorted. To change height and width independently turn Constrain Proportions off. The point to remember is that this command affects every layer.

To control the resolution of the resulting image, check Resample Image and one of the following:

– *Bicubic Smoother:* when enlarging image size

– *Bicubic Sharper:* when reducing image size to maintain detail (If it oversharpens some areas, switch to Bicubic.)

– *Bicubic:* slow but more precise method that results in the smoothest tonal gradations

– *Nearest Neighbor or Bilinear:* We don't recommend using either. Click OK.

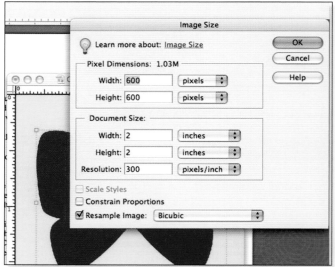

Changing the dimensions of the workspace and all layers with Image Size

2. **Use the Crop tool** <c>.

Modify the size and shape of all layers in a file in either Standard Edit or Quick Fix modes. The simplest approach is to select the tool, drag the cursor across the workspace to roughly outline the area to keep, and then fine-tune the selections by moving the selection box around or changing one or more sides. Press <ENTER> or double click to accept. The Crop Tool Options bar that appears above the workspace allows you to easily control this process using the Custom pull-down menu. For example, if you select one of the height-to-width ratios listed, the bounding box will maintain those proportions as you drag it over your image. A handy way of changing the current workspace to one with a specific dimension and resolution is to type new values in the boxes on the Crop Options bar. Using the Custom Option of the Crop tool can result in a larger image as easily as a smaller image, a seeming contradiction.

Resize or rotate an object in a layer

The following information focuses on changing the dimensions of an object or selected area on one layer; the workspace size will not be affected, nor will objects on other layers. These tools are used to increase or decrease the size of or rotate whatever is selected. In some cases, part of the image may extend beyond the limits of the workspace (and, thus, beyond view). However, the rest of it is still there if you need it.

1. **Use Free Transform.**

Select the layer that contains a shape created with the Cookie Cutter. Be sure the Move tool (v) is selected and click on the bounding box that appears. You could also select [Image> Transform>Free Transform] or press <CTRL t>. Increase or decrease the dimensions of the object proportionally (drag a corner) or reshape it by dragging just one side of the box. When you are satisfied press <ENTER> (v4.0) or click [✓] (v 5.0, v6.0, v7.0). Look at the boxes on the left of the Free Transform Options bar to check whether you have

Changing the dimensions of one object using Free Transform

maintained the original aspect ratio of the selection. If you hold down the Shift key when dragging the corner of the bounding box around an image, it will maintain the original aspect ratio of the image.

The Free Transform Options bar

2. **Freely rotate a layer.**

With the Move tool (v) and the layer selected, move the cursor until it is just OUTSIDE the boundary box and click. Gradually rotate the layer around, or you can type a percentage into the set rotate box in the Free Transform Options bar.

3. **Change the percent.**

Alternatively, you can type a percent change into the appropriate box in the Free Transform Options bar. The original aspect ratio will be maintained if you enter the same value for width and height. It will be distorted vertically or horizontally if the values are different. Above, the butterfly width was reduced to 75% of the original. Press <ENTER> (v4.0) or click [✓] (v5.0, 6.0, v7.0) to effect the change. This is the same option bar that appears during the second stage of cutting a cookie.

The Image/Rotate menu used to flip the entire workspace

Rotate or flip an appliqué

If you don't like the orientation of a shape after you cut it with the Cookie Cutter tool, you can easily change it using the Rotate pull-down menu [Image>Rotate]. The upper group of options will affect all of the layers in that file, flipping or rotating every-thing at once with a single command. In the previous illustration, we simply flipped the image horizontally [Image>Rotate>Flip Horizontal], although we could have turned it upside down or rotated it to the right or left by the degrees specified in the Custom Option submenu.

The Image/Rotate menu used to flip an appliqué on just one layer

Rotate a layer or object on a layer

The lower group of options in the Rotate menu are applied to the selected layer (or object) only, such as the group of flowers in the example. [Image>Rotate>Layer 90° Left or Right, 180°, Flip Horizontal or Vertical]. These commands are handy when you need to create different orientations of the same shape by copying and rotating, rather than cutting different versions of the same shape.

> **Hint**
>
> It is easy to forget to press <ENTER> when you are finished resizing, rotating, or flipping an object. Until you do this simple step, Photoshop Elements will simply ignore you. So, when nothing seems to be working, press <ENTER>.

MORE ABOUT LAYERS

Think of layers as pieces of fabric, pieced blocks, or appliquéd shapes, placed on layers of glass that are stacked one on top of the other. In the next example, the background and shapes, each cut from a piece of Digital Stash created with the Mosaic Filter, are different layers. Pieces of fabric are independent until you sew them; the layers are independent until you merge them. You can change color or bright-ness, apply layer styles, add filters, and change opacity on only one layer without affecting the others, just like you can with pieces of fabric. The top portion of the next example on page 19 shows a conceptual illustration of the layers required to make a pieced Diamond-in-a-Square block, how they look in the Photoshop Elements workspace, and how they stack in the Layers palette.

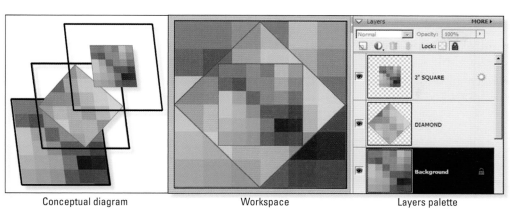

| Conceptual diagram | Workspace | Layers palette |

The bottom portion of the example at the left shows the Layers palette diagram on a Photoshop Elements 6 screen. It uses the layers from the pieced block below, adds an appliqué cookie shape on top of the Diamond and Background layers, and hides the 2" square layer. The new Hue/Saturation adjustment layer on top changes the block color to more of an orange and brown hue. Adjustment layers like the Hue/Saturation and Invert Adjustment layers let you play with color and other adjustments without permanently modifying layers below it. Refer to the Color Play section on pages 31–35 for more information on using these adjustment layers.

To view layers in the Palette Bin, select [Window>Layers].

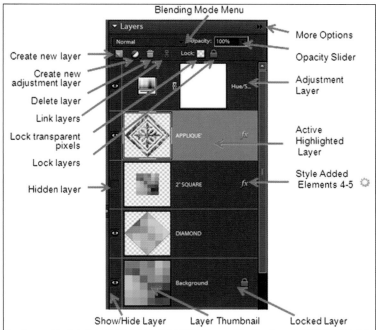

Hint

You should always have the Layers palette visible.

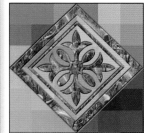

Appliqué block

Using Layer commands

Where do you find the layer commands?
– *Layer menu*
– *Icons on the Layers palette* (identified above)
– *Right click* (PC) or *control click* (Mac) on a layer in the Layers palette
– *Click on More Options or Double Arrows* in the Layers palette top right corner

The commands on pages 20–21 help you manage your layers, explaining how to create new layers, or rearrange, duplicate, delete, or merge them. Knowing how to manipulate layers is essential, so make sure you know how to use the commands. To select the layer you want to work on, click on its name (in the Layers palette) or on some part of an object that is on that layer. Photoshop Elements 4 and 5 highlight the active (selected) layer in blue; Photoshop Elements 6 and 7 highlight the active layer in light grey.

After you create or change a layer, take a second to double click on the name and rename it to something meaningful, so you can manage your layers more easily. When you apply a filter, you could list the filter name and key values. Before you choose a command, make sure you have selected the layer you wish to change and it is visible.

Refer to Resize, Rotate & Flip on pages 16–18 for more information on resizing, rotating, and flipping layers.

- **Move and hide layers.**

   To change the layer stacking order, move a layer up or down:

   – *Click on and then drag the layer* up or down in the Layers Bin or

   – *Select* [Layer>Arrange] or

   – *Click* (PC, right click) on an object on that layer in the workspace.

   Show or hide layers by clicking on the "eye" next to the layer.

- **Create a new layer.**

   The easiest way to create a new blank layer is to click on the Create New Layer symbol at the top left of the Layers Bin or press <CTRL SHIFT n>. You can paint the new layer with a Paint Bucket color or pattern, and use it as a background or cut a cookie shape from it.

- **Duplicate a layer.**

   Duplicating a layer before cutting a cookie shape, or applying a filter or layer styles, is a great way to try new things and compare them with the original layer. If you create a filter and want to keep it, you still have the original to use. The easiest way to duplicate a layer is to click on it and press <CTRL j>.

   – *Copy* <CTRL c> *and Paste* <CTRL v> something from the active layer in this or another file and it will be pasted into a new layer in the same or a different file.

   – *Copy Merged* combines the screen view of all the visible layers into one new layer without altering the original layers.

   Select all layers [Select>All Layers] or press <CTRL a> then select [Edit>Copy Merged] or press <SHIFT CTRL c>. Paste into a new layer in the same or a different file.

   You could also select [File>New>Image from Clipboard] to paste into a new file. This is a quick way to copy a completed block or background into a new file.

Hint

Clicking on an object to select that individual layer only works if the "Auto Select Layer" option (on the top left of the Move menu bar) is checked.

- **Merge visible layers.**

   Select [Layers>Merge Visible], <CTRL SHIFT e> or [Layer Palette>More>Merge Visible]. It will ignore layers that are not visible. Merging all the visible layers can make managing your layers easier and reduces the file size.

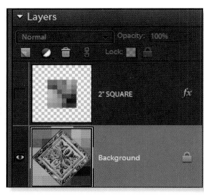

Result after Merge Visible on appliqué block layers in previous example. Because the 2" square was hidden, it was not merged.

- **Merge down.**

   Select [Layer>Merge Down] or press <CTRL e> to combine the selected visible layer with an unlocked visible layer directly below it.

   The example below shows the result of Merge Down applied on the top adjustment layer (Hue/Saturation) in the diagram on the previous page. The background has switched back to green because the adjustment layer (Hue/Saturation) was merged with the appliqué layer and now only changes the appliqué layer.

Merge Down applied to top Hue/Saturation layer

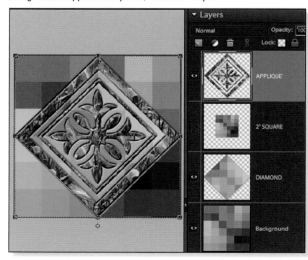

- **Delete a layer.**

   Drag the layer to the trash can icon at the top of the Layers palette to delete a layer. Note: You could delete the 2" square layer because it is hidden.

- **Change layer opacity.**

   Drag the Opacity slider to make a layer more transparent and then see how the results combine with the layer below. At least one way to use opacity is explained in the Digital Stash section for blending layers. Create two layers and play with opacity. You can create some great effects.

- **Save layers.**

   To retain the layers, save the file as Photoshop filename.psd. Photoshop Elements automatically flattens all layers when it saves as a JPEG file.

- **Choose more options.**

   Located at the top right corner of the Layers palette, the More Options or Double Arrows icon accesses many of the layer commands listed above. Click on layer options to change the thumbnail size. If you have many layers and want to see them, make the thumbnail size smaller and more layers will appear.

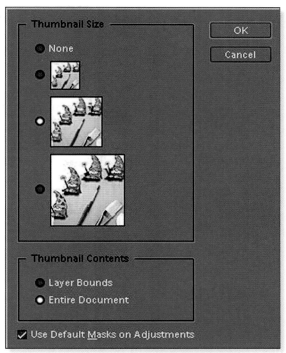

More options thumbnail size

- **Another example:**

   The Layers palette shows how layers display with a thumbnail size of none. The Rose background layer is duplicated and filtered with the wave filter, then lightened with the Hue/Saturation adjustment layer. The foreground consists of three stacked cookie shapes and two more Hue/Saturation adjustment layers.

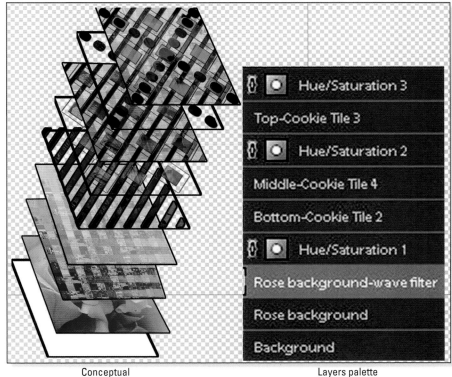

Conceptual   Layers palette

DIGITAL STASH

If you want to make digital quilts, you will need a Digital Stash. But don't head for the store! You can make all of the fabric you will need using your own photographs as starting points. Think of the resulting digital files as "fat quarters" that you can make and change whenever you choose. Because your own pictures are the starting points, your quilts will be completely unique and personal in a way not possible with commercial fabric. The best part is that each of the "fat quarters" you create can be used over and over. The only cost is your time and a little computer disk space.

The following steps will get you started. As you learn more about Photoshop Elements, however, you will discover new ways to apply one or more techniques so your fabric becomes a work of art itself.

Choosing and preparing images

Select several photographs that have pleasing colors and a range of textures and shades. They might include leaves, favorite flowers, interesting buildings, beautiful skies, or close-ups of natural textures such as bark, rocks, water, bird wings, etc. If they are printed on paper, scan them at 300 ppi and set the shortest side of the output to 8".

Open the first digital image in Photoshop Elements [File>Open] or <CTRL o>. Crop it <c> to eliminate extraneous details and adjust its size and resolution using [Image>Resize>Image size] or press <CTRL ALT i>. We usually work with images that are 7" or 8" wide at 240 – 300 ppi resolution. Now is the time to enhance image contrast, saturation, sharpness, hue, exposure, and so on if you need to, using either Quick Fix or other tools.

Applying filters

Begin experimenting with filters. If you do not like what happens you can always back up by selecting [Edit>Undo], pressing <CTRL z>, or moving up a few steps in Undo History and trying something else. Photoshop Elements is VERY forgiving so play around. You can choose from the list in the Filters menu, Filters Gallery, or from the thumbnail depiction of what each filter does in the Palette Bin on the right side of the workspace:

Photoshop Elements v4.0: Styles & Effects Palette> Filters Palette

Photoshop Elements v5.0: Artwork & Effects Palette> Apply Effects, Filters and Layers Styles>Filters

Photoshop Elements v6.0, v7.0: Effects Palette> Filters Palette

Since not all filters are visible in the Filter Gallery, we use either the Filters menu or the Filters palette to find everything that is available. Sandy finds it easier to set the displayed filters in the palette to "all" because she can never remember which filter is in which submenu.

Select the layer to which you wish to apply a filter and then double click on the little icon of the filter to be applied. You may need to supply additional information before the magic happens. Play around with different combinations of filters and types of images to see what happens when you change the values. Many filters provide a preview window so you can see the effects of your current choices on your image.

Examples of what filters can do

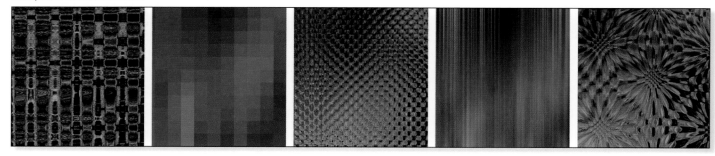

Bas Relief

Colored Pencil

Extrude

This table describes our favorite filters with an example of how the screen might look as you apply each one. On the following pages, we apply each filter to different types of images to get your creative juices flowing — a fairly monochromatic close-up of leaves with sharply defined edges, a close-up of a flower with contrasting leaves and background, and a sunrise with subtle textures but lots of color variation. When you begin to add filters to your own images, play around with the values to get the effect that works best with that image and creates the effect you intended.

Bas Relief (Sketch submenu)
Creates beautiful, textured background fabric of any color or white-on-white effects with subtle textures and shades. It emphasizes an image's edges and textures while replacing its original colors with the foreground and background colors. In the examples, we used Beige/White, White/Blue, and two shades selected from the original image with the Color Picker. We generally set Detail to the maximum (15), Smoothness to the minimum (1), and select the Light Source that produces the best effect.

Colored Pencil (Artistic submenu)
The Colored Pencil filter creates an outline of the image on a solid white, gray, or black background (paper brightness) and fills it with pencil strokes in colors taken from the image itself, giving a cross-hatch appearance. Pencil Width and Stroke Pressure influence how bright or delicate/bold the result looks. Pencil Widths in the examples ranged from 8 – 17, Stroke Pressure = 15, and Paper Brightness was 28 or 0.

Extrude (Stylize submenu)
Creates a 3D, faceted effect using colors and contrasts in the image. The *Blocks* option creates rectangular projections while the *Pyramids* option creates pointed projections. The *Size* and *Depth* options determine the number and size of the projections. *Random* creates arbitrary depths while *Level-based* uses light/dark in the image — bright objects protrude more than dark. We used values of 255, 20, and Random in the examples.

	Original	Bas Relief	Colored Pencil	Extrude
LEAF				
HYDRANGEA				
SUNRISE				

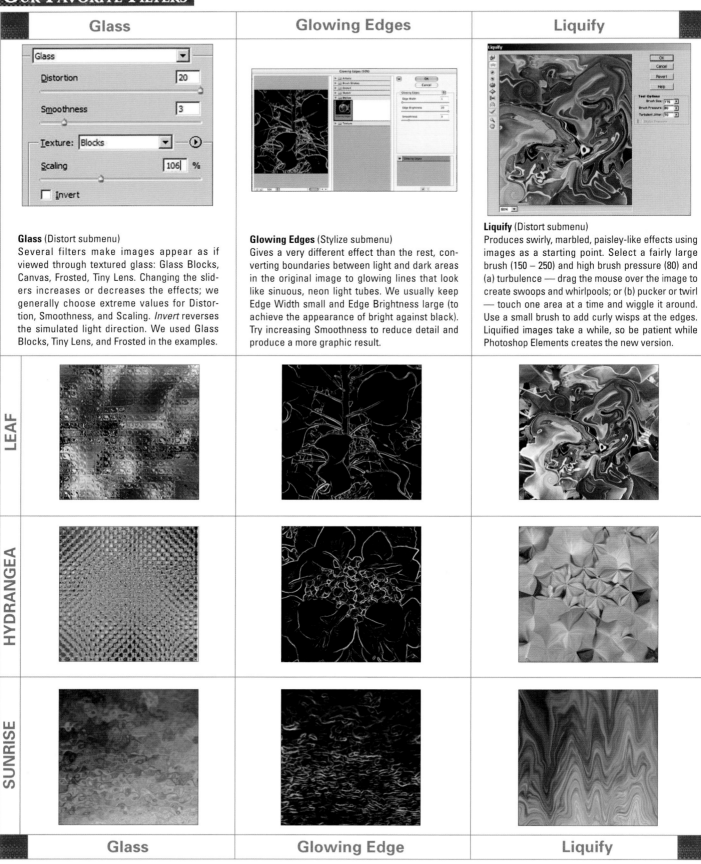

Glass

Glass (Distort submenu)
Several filters make images appear as if viewed through textured glass: Glass Blocks, Canvas, Frosted, Tiny Lens. Changing the sliders increases or decreases the effects; we generally choose extreme values for Distortion, Smoothness, and Scaling. *Invert* reverses the simulated light direction. We used Glass Blocks, Tiny Lens, and Frosted in the examples.

Glowing Edges

Glowing Edges (Stylize submenu)
Gives a very different effect than the rest, converting boundaries between light and dark areas in the original image to glowing lines that look like sinuous, neon light tubes. We usually keep Edge Width small and Edge Brightness large (to achieve the appearance of bright against black). Try increasing Smoothness to reduce detail and produce a more graphic result.

Liquify

Liquify (Distort submenu)
Produces swirly, marbled, paisley-like effects using images as a starting point. Select a fairly large brush (150 – 250) and high brush pressure (80) and (a) turbulence — drag the mouse over the image to create swoops and whirlpools; or (b) pucker or twirl — touch one area at a time and wiggle it around. Use a small brush to add curly wisps at the edges. Liquified images take a while, so be patient while Photoshop Elements creates the new version.

LEAF

HYDRANGEA

SUNRISE

Glass | Glowing Edge | Liquify

Mosaic	Motion Blur	Offset

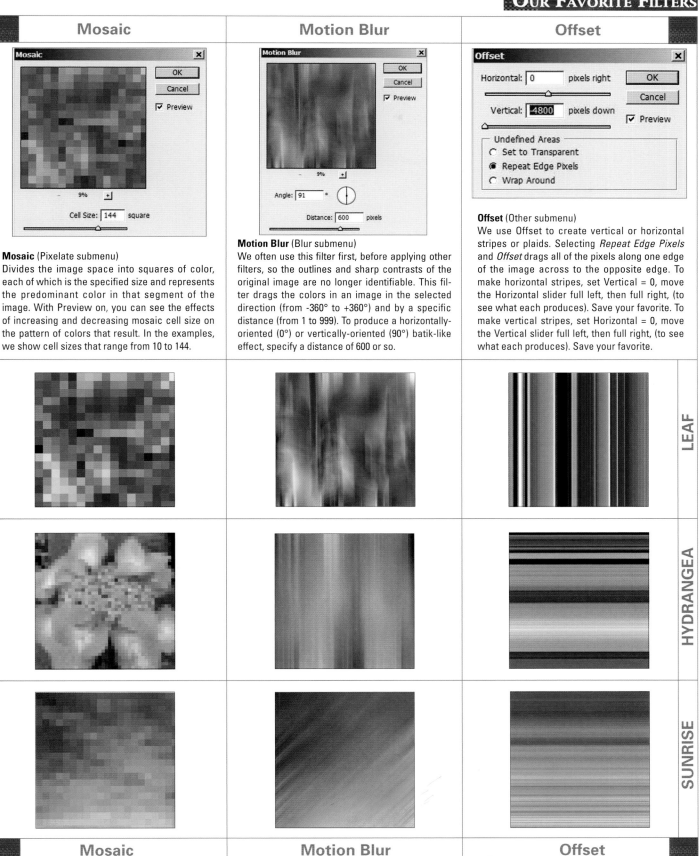

Mosaic (Pixelate submenu)
Divides the image space into squares of color, each of which is the specified size and represents the predominant color in that segment of the image. With Preview on, you can see the effects of increasing and decreasing mosaic cell size on the pattern of colors that result. In the examples, we show cell sizes that range from 10 to 144.

Motion Blur (Blur submenu)
We often use this filter first, before applying other filters, so the outlines and sharp contrasts of the original image are no longer identifiable. This filter drags the colors in an image in the selected direction (from -360° to +360°) and by a specific distance (from 1 to 999). To produce a horizontally-oriented (0°) or vertically-oriented (90°) batik-like effect, specify a distance of 600 or so.

Offset (Other submenu)
We use Offset to create vertical or horizontal stripes or plaids. Selecting *Repeat Edge Pixels* and *Offset* drags all of the pixels along one edge of the image across to the opposite edge. To make horizontal stripes, set Vertical = 0, move the Horizontal slider full left, then full right, (to see what each produces). Save your favorite. To make vertical stripes, set Horizontal = 0, move the Vertical slider full left, then full right, (to see what each produces). Save your favorite.

Mosaic	Motion Blur	Offset

LEAF

HYDRANGEA

SUNRISE

OUR FAVORITE FILTERS

Pointillize	Radial Blur	Shear

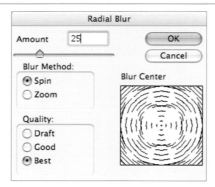

Pointillize (Pixelate submenu)
Creates subtle tone-on-tone effects where the individual dots are only visible upon close inspection; or cheerful, high-contrast polka-dot images filled with large, multicolored shapes. It captures all of the colors in the image and fills the workspace with multi-hued, multi-sided "dots" of the specified size. It uses the background color (check the little squares at the bottom of the toolbar) to color the area between the dots. The cell sizes in the examples range from 18 to 36 on either white or black backgrounds.

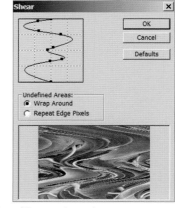

Radial Blur (Blur submenu)
Images filtered with a Radial Blur make particularly nice centers for circular shapes; it gives the effect of looking at an image through a piece of thick bulls-eye glass. The greater the amount of blur, the smoother and less recognizable the end result will be — we used the *Spin* method with values from 25% to 100% from left to right. Try *Zoom* and see if you like it, too. Use the *Draft* setting to audition different values, then *Best* for the final version.

Shear (Distort submenu)
Create fabric with a marbled effect by distorting the image along a curve that you create by clicking on the vertical line in the middle of the window in the pop-up screen. You can drag existing points to adjust the degree of distortion and add additional curve points. Try both *Wrap Around* and *Repeat Edge Pixels* to see which you prefer.

LEAF

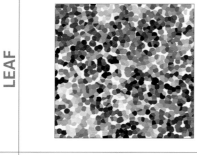

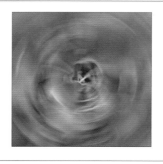

HYDRANGEA

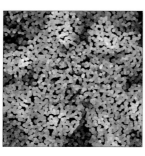

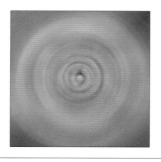

SUNRISE

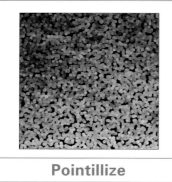

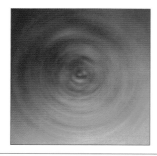

Pointillize	Radial Blur	Shear

Tiles | Wave (Sine) | Wave (Square)

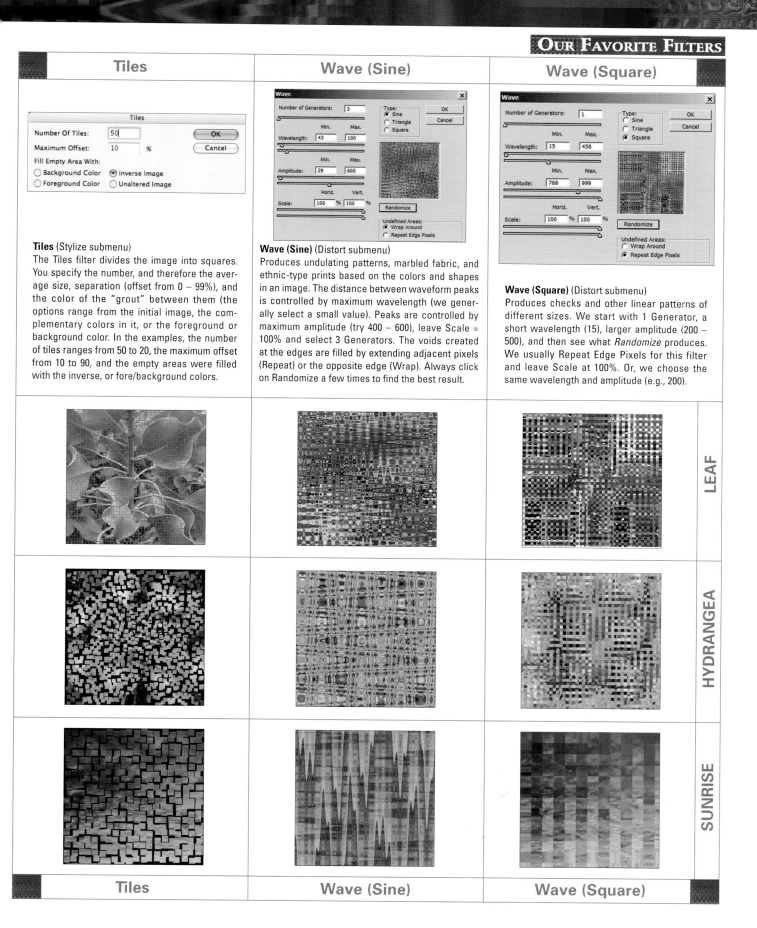

Tiles (Stylize submenu)
The Tiles filter divides the image into squares. You specify the number, and therefore the average size, separation (offset from 0 – 99%), and the color of the "grout" between them (the options range from the initial image, the complementary colors in it, or the foreground or background color. In the examples, the number of tiles ranges from 50 to 20, the maximum offset from 10 to 90, and the empty areas were filled with the inverse, or fore/background colors.

Wave (Sine) (Distort submenu)
Produces undulating patterns, marbled fabric, and ethnic-type prints based on the colors and shapes in an image. The distance between waveform peaks is controlled by maximum wavelength (we generally select a small value). Peaks are controlled by maximum amplitude (try 400 – 600), leave Scale = 100% and select 3 Generators. The voids created at the edges are filled by extending adjacent pixels (Repeat) or the opposite edge (Wrap). Always click on Randomize a few times to find the best result.

Wave (Square) (Distort submenu)
Produces checks and other linear patterns of different sizes. We start with 1 Generator, a short wavelength (15), larger amplitude (200 – 500), and then see what *Randomize* produces. We usually Repeat Edge Pixels for this filter and leave Scale at 100%. Or, we choose the same wavelength and amplitude (e.g., 200).

LEAF

HYDRANGEA

SUNRISE

Tiles | Wave (Sine) | Wave (Square)

Recycle the good ones

If you like a pattern, but it isn't the color you need, you can easily modify it as described in Color Play, pages 31–35. From one really great texture, you can create a whole palette of new digital fabrics that are lighter or darker, more or less saturated, or different combinations of colors than the original. We show only one example, although the possibilities are endless.

CALIFORNIA SUNRISES exemplifies another, related approach to modifying Digital Stash; rather than applying Hue/Saturation to an entire layer, select one part of it using the Marquee tool or the Polygon Lasso tool and alter just that section. The quilt in the example is composed of four 9-patch blocks composed of 2" squares cut from the Digital Stash based on a glorious California sunrise photo. To add a little interest, half-square triangles are outlined on top of four squares in each block using the Polygon Lasso tool. The color of just this area is altered using Hue/Saturation. This gives the appearance of pieced half-square triangles with little effort.

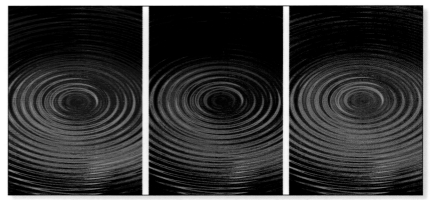

Playing around with Hue/Saturation to increase Digital Stash options

CALIFORNIA SUNRISES, 12" x 12". Created and owned by Sandy Hart, 2007. It was printed on Color Textiles broadcloth using an Epson Stylus R1800 printer.

Hint

When adding filters to duplicate copies of a photo on different layers of one file, it helps to move the layer you are working on to the top of the stack or make the other layers invisible by clicking on their "eyes."

Save the good ones

When you find an effect that you like, save the resulting image as a JPEG file [File>Save As >filename.jpg] or <CTRL SHIFT s>. You might want to keep a record of how you produced transformations that you particularly like so you can try the same settings with another image in the future. After applying different filters or combinations of filters to one image, move onto the next until you have an array of colors and textures.

Organize your Digital Stash

If you get as hooked as we have on making Digital Stash out of every interesting image that you can, remembering what you have made (and where they are saved) requires a bit of organization.

There are at least two approaches that you can take to ensure that your Digital Stash is easy to access in the future:

1. Gudny duplicates the original image several times in one file and applies filters to each of the copies on their separate layers. She names these layers with the filter and settings used. Then, she saves all of these variations in a single PSD file labeled with the name of the original image (e.g., Sunrise.psd).

2. Sandy saves each transformation as a separate JPEG file labeled with the name of the image and the filter(s) applied (e.g., Sunrise-Tiles.jpg, Sunrise-Extrude.jpg). She saves these files in labeled folders organized by topic, project, or any other organizational scheme that helps her find the work of art that is just what she needs for the current project. This may not seem important when you are in the throes of your first creative rush, but you will be glad you spent a little time getting organized the first time a special creation strays into a remote area of your computer and disappears forever. As your Digital Stash grows, you might consider printing **CONTACT SHEETS** that show thumbnails of each one, if you save your stash as JPEGS. **MAC:** [File>Contact Sheet 2] or <CTRL OPT p>; **PC:** [File>Print Multiple Photos] or <CTRL ALT p> (Organizer opens) [Select Type of Print>Contact Sheets].

Multiple filters

You have made stripes, dots, checks, "batiks," and lots of other incredible textured fabric. Now try applying more than one filter before you save the results for even more interesting effects. As you apply successive filters, the results will become more abstract until the subject of the original image subject is no longer identifiable. Sandy likes a more abstract effect, so she usually applies Motion Blur first and then adds other filters on top of it. Tiny Lens is another favorite as it adds a little sparkle to the results of other filters.

You can repeat the same filter to get different results. For example, adding a horizontally-oriented Motion Blur on top of a vertically-oriented Motion Blur can create a "solid" fabric with subtle gradations. If you repeat the Tiles filter several times with different background and foreground colors you get different colored tiles.

The three examples, right, show successive applications of Motion Blur, Sine Wave, Colored Pencil, Tiny Lens, Mosaic, and Liquify, although we could have presented any number of other combinations. Because each filter is added to the results of the preceding filter, the image continues to occupy one layer and can be easily saved as a JPEG.

Gudny particularly likes the Extrude and Shear filters because they create wavy effects. In the example below, Gudny applied the Extrude filter to a blue sky photo with many clouds. Then, she applied a Shear filter over the results of that and added color using Hue/Saturation. Before she printed four copies of the results, she rotated or flipped them and further modified the colors slightly.

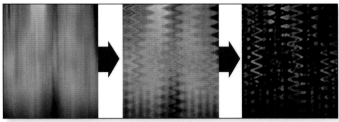

Multiple Filters: Hydrangea close-up filtered with Blur (Motion Blur); Distort (Sine Wave); Artistic (Colored Pencil)

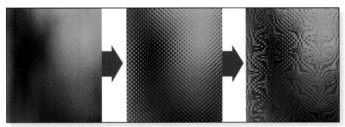

Multiple Filters: Photo of colored Easter eggs filtered with Blur (Motion Blur); Distort/Glass (Tiny Lens); and then Liquify (Pinch tool)

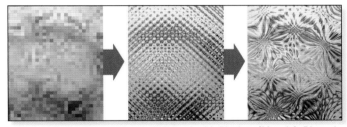

Multiple Filters: Photo of a shell filtered with Pixelate (Mosaic); Distort/Glass (Tiny Lens); and then Distort/Liquify (Pinch tool)

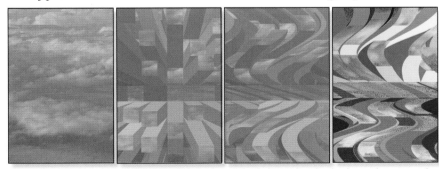

Four steps to create a complex "fabric" from the original photo of a cloudy sky, to the successive additions of Extrude then Shear filters with color added using Hue/Saturation

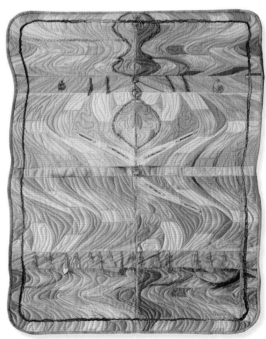

CLOUDS, 22" x 28". Created and owned by Gudny Campbell, 2007. Printed on silk treated with Bubble Jet Set on an Epson Stylus® R1800 printer.

Blended fabric

Another option is to stack filtered layers on top of one another in a single file. If the opacity of the top layer is reduced (e.g., between 40 to 75%), the contents of the

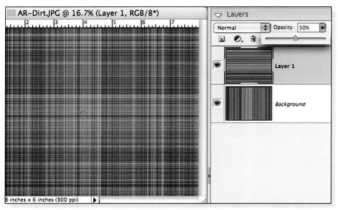

Plaid from stripes created with the Offset filter (in the Other submenu)

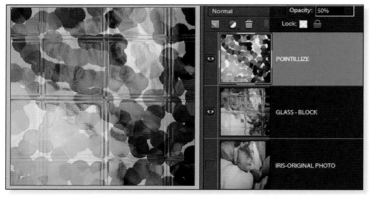

Blended Layers—a close-up photo of an iris filtered with Distort/Glass (Glass Block) and Pixelate (Pointillize)

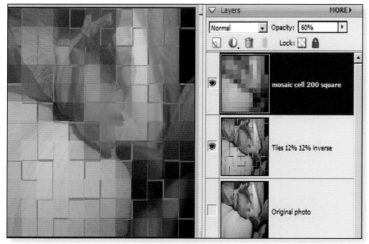

Blended layers—one copy is filtered with Pixelate (Mosaic), the other with Stylize (Tile)

Hint

When applying filters found in the Effects palette that have a Preview Image in the pop-up menu, zoom out until you can view the whole image.

bottom layer show through the top layer giving the effect of placing patterned sheer fabric on top of opaque fabric. A layer's opacity determines whether it reveals the layer beneath it; a layer with 1% opacity is nearly transparent, while a layer with 100% opacity is completely opaque.

The first example shows a plaid fabric based on a picture of red clay taken in Arkansas. First, vertical stripes are created using the Offset filter, found in the Filters palette. After duplicating the layer <CTRL j>, the topmost version is rotated 90° [Image >Rotate>Layer 90° Left or Right]. Since the new layer doesn't cover the original, its size is increased using Free Transform [Image>Free Transform] or <CTRL t>. Then, the magic happens — when the opacity of the top layer is reduced to 50%, plaid appears! The two layers can be merged by selecting the top layer and then [Layer>Merge Down] or <CTRL e>. Once the layers are merged, the contents of the two layers will be completely blended and can be saved as a "plaid" version of the original image by selecting [File>Save As] or <CTRL SHIFT s>.

The second example starts with a close-up photo of an iris. The top layer is filtered with Glass Blocks and its opacity is reduced to 70%. The second copy of the iris photo is filtered with Pointillize using a large Cell Size (225). (The original photo was 8" square, but was cropped and reduced in size to illustrate the process.)

The third example, also based on the same 8" close-up of an iris, illustrates the effects of blending duplicate layers modified by Mosaic or Tile filters. After making the Mosaic layer, Gudny counted the number of rows of squares (12 in the example) and entered that value when specifying the Number of Tiles and Tiles Offset % when applying the Tiles filter to the second copy of the photo. In the example, she used Inverse Image to fill the empty areas that were created. When you try this on your own, move the Mosaic layer above the Tiles layer and reduce its opacity to around 60% so you can see both.

Color Play

Have you ever found a wonderful fabric but wished it were slightly lighter or darker, or blue instead of yellow? Do you want to change your photo to make the grass greener, or a flower purple instead of red? Using Photoshop Elements you can very easily adjust colors.

What are the basic color terms?

Hue – The name of the color such as red, orange, or green

Saturation – The color's strength; fully saturated contains no gray. Saturation is decreased by adding white or black.

Lightness and brightness – The aspect of color related to intensity or value

Contrast – The difference in brightness between light and dark areas

Complement – The opposite value of a color on the color wheel that contrasts in the most extreme way.

The example below illustrates the basic color terms:

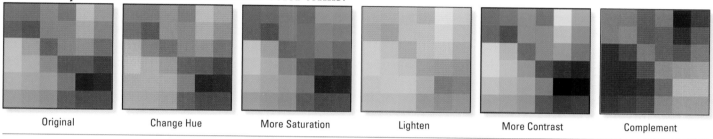

Original   Change Hue   More Saturation   Lighten   More Contrast   Complement

When should you change colors?

You can change colors at any time — when you first open a blank, photo, or Digital Stash file; after you cut a cookie shape or create a background layer; or at the end on a completed block.

View your completed block or quilt as if it were hanging on a design wall. Zoom out to view it as though you were looking from a distance or with a reducing glass. Use this perspective to fine-tune your colors. Be sure there is enough contrast between the cookie shape(s) and the background. If any of the colors clash, change them.

If you will be printing one block multiple times to make a quilt, consider changing the appearance of each copy of the block (or an element of it) to be a little darker or lighter.

Four tools to change color

Paint Bucket – Fill areas with a solid color or pattern.

Color Variations – Correct color by comparing thumbnail variations of midtones, highlights, shadows, or saturation. A preview screen showing before and after images is a very handy way to create fabric gradations.

Hue/Saturation – Change the hue, saturation, or lightness of one or multiple layers. Use it to change only one color or several, one at a time. Preview any adjustments you make on the image itself.

Invert – Change the color to its color wheel complement.

Paint Bucket tool

The Paint Bucket fills areas with a solid color using the foreground color, or patterns on one or more layers, or in a marquee selection. Note that the Paint Bucket Options bar looks slightly different between Photoshop Elements 4 and 5 and Photoshop Elements 6 and 7.

- **Choose a blending mode.**
  The Paint Bucket has a Blending Mode menu that offers many options, but for all of the examples in this book we use "Normal."

- **Thin the paint.**
  The Paint Bucket opacity slider allows you to "thin the paint." At 100%, the coverage is complete. At 50% or less, the color wash you add will blend with or only tint what is already there.

Paint Bucket Options bars for:
Photoshop Elements v4.0 and v5.0

Photoshop Elements
v6.0 and v7.0

- **Adjust the tolerance.**

For Tolerance, specify a low percentage to replace colors very similar to the color you select or raise the percentage to replace a broader range of colors. The nominal setting is 25, although you can replace this with a value from 0 to 255; higher numbers cause a broader range of shades to be included.

- **Smooth the edges.**

Anti-Alias smoothes the edges of the fill color slightly. We keep it on.

- **Select the Contiguous option.**

The Contiguous option controls whether the fill is applied to adjacent areas only. If Contiguous is on, the Paint Bucket will fill only the area (or color) you selected until it touches a different color. If it is off, it will fill every place with that color.

- **Use All Layers.**

The Use All Layers checkbox allows you to fill all layers at once.

- **Select foreground fill color.**

The foreground color is what will fill a Paint Bucket or brush. The current values for foreground and background colors may be seen in two tiny boxes at the lower left of the tool bar. There are several different ways to change its value:

– *Click on the Foreground color square* at the bottom of the toolbar *and use the Color Picker*.

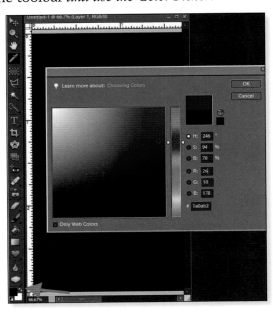

When the Color Picker screen appears, modify the current foreground color by clicking somewhere in the color space or select a different color from the rainbow slider to the right. Select the color of your choice by clicking on OK, and then fill the shape using the Paint Bucket tool.

– *Click a swatch* in the Window>Color Swatches palette.

– *Hold down the Alt key and click on an area on your image.* The eyedropper symbol appears and the foreground is changed to this color.

The following examples show the effect of setting the Tolerance to 50 and turning the Contiguous settings on and off when coloring with the Paint Bucket tool. The foreground color is yellow. The square clicked on is highlighted in black.

Controlling color

You control how much is colored by **changing the Tolerance and Contiguous settings.** The best way to understand is to try it. Open an image and set the foreground color to something not in your image. Start with a Tolerance of 5 and Contiguous on. Repeat several times, increasing the tolerance and turning contiguous on and off, ending with a Tolerance of 255 and Contiguous off. Undo <CTRL z> after you change the settings so you recolor the original image over and over.

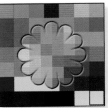 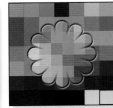

Original block   Background layer, Contiguous off   Background layer, Contiguous on

In the last example, setting the Tolerance to 255 and Contiguous off colors the whole cookie shape layer with the foreground color.

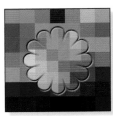 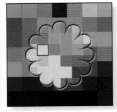 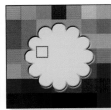

Cookie shape layer, Contiguous on   Cookie shape layer, Contiguous off   Cookie shape layer, Tolerance 255, Contiguous off

Selecting pattern fill

In the Paint Bucket options bar in Photoshop Elements 6 and 7, click on the pattern checkbox; in Photoshop Elements 4 and 5, change the foreground pull down menu to pattern. The pattern pull down menu appears just to the right. Select a pattern to use and click on the area you want to recolor. Photoshop Elements includes a library of patterns that are useful in combination with blending modes. The creativity is in creating your own patterns.

To define a new pattern, open an image or make a selection using the Rectangular Marquee tool, then select [Edit>Define Pattern]. The pattern appears at the bottom of the pattern pulldown menu in the Paint Bucket.

Consider the following issues and alternatives when managing your patterns:

– *Tiling issues:* If the pattern size is smaller than the shape or layer size, it will create multiple copies called tiles. If the pattern size is bigger, it will only show part of the pattern. This is a common problem, especially with real images like the butterfly in the first example. Small abstract textures work better.

– *Transparent Patterns:* All the previous examples show solid patterns; however you can make patterns with transparent parts. The only restriction is that the selection has to be rectangular. The highlighted layer is a 4" square pattern created from the Mosaic filter. Use the Magic Wand to delete every other square, then select a square area so the top left and bottom right are filled in. Resize it; then select [Edit>Define Pattern]. When you use the pattern, create a new layer and color it with the Paint Bucket pattern. Add a layer below it and change the pattern layer opacity to around 70%.

– *Adjustment Layer Patterns*: Try another way to use a Paint Bucket pattern on a layer. Click on the Create Adjustment Layer icon in the Layers palette, and then select Pattern. The Pattern Fill menu appears and you can scale the pattern size. The pattern fills the layer at the scale you selected. This is great for adding borders.

In the examples below, the pattern doesn't show correctly. The Square-in-a-Square block doesn't fit correctly in the diamonds of the cookie shape.

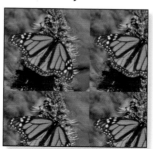

A 2½" square butterfly pattern is applied to a 4" square layer. Parts of three butterflies are missing.

A 4" square pattern is applied to an 8" square cookie. Each diamond is different. The background pattern is more textural.

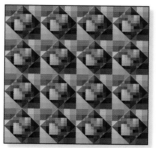
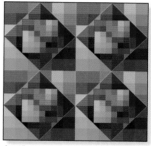

A 2" square block pattern is applied to an 8" square layer.

A 4" square pattern is applied to an 8" square layer.

The examples above look okay. The 2" pattern is ¼ of an 8" block, and the 4" pattern is ½. You could quickly duplicate a block by defining the pattern with a size that is a percentage of the whole block.

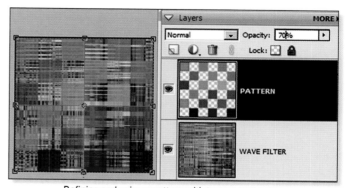

Defining and using a pattern with transparent parts

Preset Manager screen showing a mix of default and user-defined patterns

– *Memory issues:* Adding patterns to the library that Photoshop Elements automatically loads every time it is launched can really lengthen the loading time if too many patterns or several really large patterns are added. Select [Edit>Preset Manager] to view and control your patterns. Photoshop Elements comes with several pattern libraries, and you can load and save your own. Project 5, Bubbles, defines a stripes pattern. The example shows a mix of Photoshop Elements default and additional favorite defined patterns, including the ones used on page 33. Keep the default set that Photoshop Elements loads small, and load other libraries as you need them. Delete patterns in a library if you don't like them. Click on the Learn More About Preset Manager link for more instructions on how to manage your patterns.

Color variations

This is the most flexible and powerful tool for modifying the appearance of a selected area or layer. To use this menu, first select the layer then select [Enhance>Adjust Color>Color Variations]. You can also outline a selection using the Marquee tool and modify just that part. The tiny thumbnails show what will happen if you select that option. You can change color by increasing or decreasing the amount of each by clicking on the thumbnail buttons one or more times. The Before and After pictures show the effect of each selection. Adjust the Color Intensity slider to the left to show more subtle changes. While in Photoshop Elements, the color intensity stays the same until you change it, which is great for making color gradations.

> Hint
>
> After you click OK, you can undo the result if you hate it.

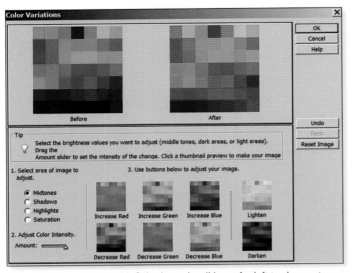

Color Variations Screen with Color Intensity slider at far left to show extreme settings. Before: original background; After: increased red.

Hue/Saturation

The Hue/Saturation command adjusts hue, saturation, and lightness on a selection, on one layer, or on one or more layers below a new adjustment layer. If the sky isn't blue enough, you can select the blue hue and only change everything blue. If you have a cookie shape and background layers and the greens don't quite match, change the green on one of the layers.

- **Adjust the Hue/Saturation.**
  On a selection or one layer, select [Enhance>Adjust Color>Adjust Hue/Saturation] or <CTRL u>.

  After you select the Hue/Saturation menu, turn Preview on so you can immediately see the results that the adjustments you make will have.

- **Create an adjustment layer.**
  Select [Layer>New Adjustment Layer>Hue/Saturation].

Click OK. This adds a new layer above the current selected layer that modifies all of the layers below without permanently changing them. If you don't like the result, hide or delete this new layer.

- **Use the Hue slider.**
Change all of the colors in an image at the same time, or change only one color at a time by selecting a specific hue to change in the Edit pull down menu.

- **Use the Saturation slider.**
Make colors more vivid or more muted. You could use this selection to add a color punch or tone down a distracting color in a specific part of an image, an entire layer, or a completed block.

- **Use the Lightness slider.**
Lighten or darken all or a selected part of an image. Experiment, and when you are happy with the result, click OK.

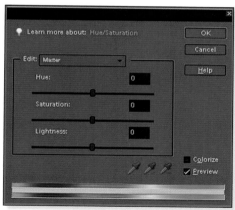

Hue/Saturation screen

 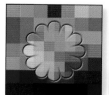 

Effects of changing hue: (left) original block; (middle) selecting magenta from the Edit pulldown menu and moving the Hue slider to the far left on the background layer (The purple in the background changes to green.); (right) creating an adjustment layer above the cookie layer and moving the master Hue slider to the right

Invert (color complement)

Change the color of a layer or several layers to its color wheel complement.

- **Create an Invert adjustment layer.**
Select [Layer>New Adjustment Layer>Invert] and click OK. This adds a new layer above the current selected layer, adjusting all the layers below without changing them. If you don't like the result, hide or delete this new layer.

- **Change one layer.**
Select the layer you want to change, then select [Layer Styles>Photographic Effects>Negative] or press <CTRL i>.

The example below shows the original block on the left; the background changed via [Layer Styles> Photographic Effects>Negative] in the middle; and the whole block inverted via an Invert adjustment layer applied above the cookie shape layer on the right.

 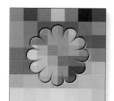 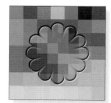

Effects of inverting the hue of layers: (left) original block; (middle) using a layer style negative on the background; (right) using the Invert adjustment layer on the block

These examples show the results of applying the color complement to a digital quilt or a background.

Effect of inverting a whole quilt: (left) before; and, (right) after

Effect of inverting the background only: (left) before; and (right) after

FROSTING

The blocks we created in the Basics section are pretty (and they took seconds to make rather than hours to appliqué or piece). However, there is so much more we could do, even with a very simple block cut from a solid color. Think about the added pizzazz that icing, sprinkles, colored sugar, and candies give a plain sugar cookie!

Examples of silhouette, outline, and stencil appliqués

In the Color Play section, we described one way to enhance an image — making part or all of it lighter, brighter, darker, or a different color. We now explore how to further embellish an image with layer styles and encourage you to play around with them at your leisure. One layer style can make all the difference to a rather bland block, while several in combination can produce dazzling results. Any layer style can be applied to the contents of any layer, whether it is "painted," a photo, or Digital Stash. Some filters affect the edges of whatever fills the layer. Others change the colors and textures that fill the layer.

Examples of typical Layer Styles palettes: Patterns, Bevels, Drop Shadows

See Layer Styles, listed in the Palette Bin under Styles and Effects (v4.0), [Artwork and Effects>Apply Filters, Effects, and Layer Styles] (v5.0), and [Effects>Layer Styles] (v6.0 and v7.0). As we play around with a few of the many ways to embellish a shape, we will demonstrate their effects on three types of shapes — a silhouette, an outline, and a stencil — filled with solid colors. Remember that similar, or even more interesting effects will be obtained with shapes cut from photos or Digital Stash.

As you select the different layer styles palettes (e.g., Bevel, Drop Shadow, Patterns) from the pull-down menu, the display area in the Effects palette will fill with squares that illustrate the effects of the options. To apply a layer style, select the layer to which it will be applied and then double click on the icon of the layer style you wish to apply. Your image will transform immediately and a little symbol will appear beside the name of that layer. If you click on this symbol, a menu will appear with options for modifying the effects of that layer style. (Notice that the little thumbnail image of the layer in the Layers palette does not change to show the effects of any layer style.) To remove all of the layer styles applied to a specific layer and start again, select [Layer>Layer Style>Clear layer style]. To remove the one you just tried, back up by pressing <CTRL z> or Undo, or re-place one layer style with another within the same category (e.g., replace an Inner Ridge with a Simple Pillow Emboss Bevel). Across type of layer styles (e.g., Bevel, Shadows, Patterns), however, you can add one on top of another. Note the different looks that layer styles give to each type of shape in the example.

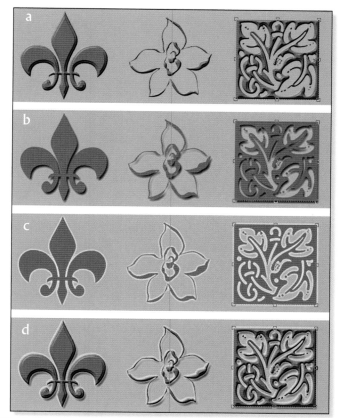

Effects of layer styles that decorate the edges of appliqués: (a) Bevel, Scalloped Edge; (b) Drop Shadow, Low; (c) Outer Glow, Simple; (d) Combination of all three

Frosting the edges

This type of layer style adds definition to the edges of a shape setting it off from the background, creating a 3D quality, and can make an otherwise bland block interesting and dramatic. All of the projects in this book frost the edges at least a little. The analogy in traditional quilting would be embroidering the edge of an appliqué; quilting in the ditch around pieced shapes; or couching bias, yarn, or ribbon.

Using Drop Shadow to create a reverse-appliqué effect

- **Audition bevels.**
We chose the Scalloped Edge Bevel for the first example [Layer Styles>Bevels>Scalloped Edge]. Audition different types of bevels to find the one you like best for a specific applique. Some create the impression that the applique is mounded slightly above the back-ground while others give the impression it is sinking down into it.

- **Use Drop Shadows.**
We chose a simple one (Low) to illustrate its effects

on different types of shapes, but you should try other alternatives. Drop Shadows sets an appliqué off from the background a little or a lot.

- **Add an Outer Glow.**
The third option we illustrate is a Simple Outer Glow that adds a bit of shine to the outer edge of a shape.

- **Try combinations.**
Finally, we combined three of the types of layer styles that frost edges. Try adding different combinations of bevels, shadows, and glows to your own appliqué.

Inner Shadows can have a wonderful effect on some combinations of appliqués and backgrounds, giving the appearance of reverse appliqué. In the example we added a Noisy Inner Shadow to the appliqués and transformed the background with the Denim layer style from Patterns.

Frosting the fabric

Other layer style menu selections change the look of the entire appliqué or background, not just the edges. It is easy to create dramatically different looks, or subtle variations, with the click of a mouse. As you play around with these types of layer styles, notice that some produce unexpected effects depending on the previously selected layer style. Imagine the creative possibilities. Want more? Add a bevel or shadow as well. We illustrate six possibilities applied to the same three appliqués, although there are dozens of other possibilities.

- **Wow Plastic** > Plastic Black
- **Patterns** > Tie-Dyed Silk
- **Patterns** > Ancient Stone
- **Image Effects** > Puzzle
- **Patterns** > Copper
- **Complex** > Paint Brush Strokes

Notice that we changed the background colors in the examples to coordinate or contrast with the transformations that we applied to the appliqués. We did this by simply selecting the layer beneath a cookie, filling the Paint Bucket with a new color, and clicking on it. Instead of solid colors, the appliqués or the background, or both, could have been filled with photos or Digital Stash adding even more interest to the result. Projects using combinations of colors from the Paint Bucket and layer styles include MOONLIT LEAVES and BUBBLES.

Combining layer styles

You can easily combine layer styles to add texture or color or create an entirely new "fabric." The background for Project 3, DOG BISCUITS, was created this way. Start with a layer style that has a lot of texture (e.g., White Grid on Orange from the Complex Palette). Then, try changing its intensity and hue by adding another layer style from Pho-

Effect of layer styles that change the appearance of the entire appliqué (plus a few bevels and shadows): (a) Wow-Black > Plastic; (b) Patterns > Tie-dyed silk; (c) Patterns > Ancient Stone; (d) Image Effects > Puzzle; (e) Patterns > Copper; (f) Complex > Paint Brush Strokes

tographic Effects to lighten it (Orange Gradient), change its hue (Purple Tone), or recolor to its complement (Negative) as shown in the first examples on page 39. The second group of examples is based on a combination of [Complex>White Grid on Orange] and [Patterns>Blanket]. Try this for yourself by creating a new layer, filling it with a Complex layer style, and then applying additional layer styles to each (e.g., Photographic/ Negative or Photographic/Blue tone) to create a collection of images that could be cut into appliqué shapes and printed on fabric.

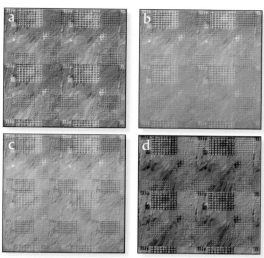

Combinations of layer styles added to a solid color layer textured with (a) Complex > Orange Grid on White; plus (b) Photographic Effects > Orange Gradient; or (c) Photographic Effects > Purple; or (d) Photographic Effects > Negative

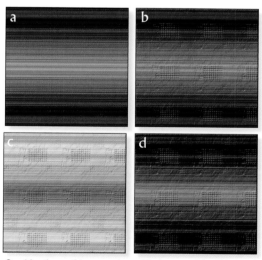

Combinations of layer styles added to a solid color layer textured with (a) Patterns > Blanket; plus (b) Complex > Orange Grid on White; or (c) Photographic Effects > Negative; or (d) Photographic Effects > Blue

Steps to making Frosted Stacks: (a) Duplicate and cut a shape from the top layer; (b) Frost with Bevels, Shadows, and Glows; (c) Lighten, darken, or recolor the shape.

Frosted stacks

Another way to use layer styles to create interesting effects is to duplicate a layer filled with paint, a photo, or Digital Stash. When you cut a shape from the top layer you can't see anything until you add a Bevel, Glow, or Shadow, as shown above. Then the magic happens — the shape simply pops from the same-image background.

Frosted Stacks from a painted layer plus: (a) Bevel; (b) Hue/Saturation; (c) Complex > Purple and Magenta

Frosted Stack from a sunrise photo

Frosted Stack from an artichoke flower close-up

With some combinations of layer fills and cookie cutter shapes, "pieced" and "appliquéd" quilt blocks emerge. As you add further embellishments, the effects become even more interesting as shown in the top group of examples. You can easily see that the tipped 9-Patch block could be created out of any number of combinations of layers filled with "paint," photos, Digital Stash, or layer styles.

The two examples, left, show how Frosted Stacks would look if the starting image was a photo. We started with a beautiful sunrise, added a cookie shape cut from the same image, and frosted it with Bevels and Shadows. The results simulate looking at the sunrise through beveled glass. The second example cuts a complex shape from a duplicate of an artichoke flower and sets it off from the background by adding Bevels and Shadows.

After the various shapes were cut from a duplicate layer, they were set apart from the background by adding Bevels, Shadows, and Glows. And then, in some cases, the color of the cut shape was modified by inverting it <CTRL i> or modifying its hue or saturation. This method of combining what you have learned so far — cutting "cookies," changing colors, and adding layer styles — on one of two identical layers offers the tools for creating a host of blocks that could be combined into dozens of interesting quilts.

Frosted Stacks from Digital Stash plus Bevels, Shadows, Glows, Invert, and/or Hue/Saturation

DIGITAL DESIGN WALL

Many of you use a flannel design wall to audition fabric and place quilt blocks. Most of the projects show you how to create digital blocks, but how do you view more than one? You will use a digital design wall to combine these blocks to view the overall project design on the computer before printing. Optionally you can add digital borders and create a digital quilt printed on fabric. You can rotate quilt blocks, put effects on top of them like appliqué, or make some of the layers more transparent. If you have an older computer with limited memory and disk space, create a smaller design wall for auditioning quilt block placement and print the individual block files separately.

Design terminology

Digital Quilt – One or more quilt blocks and an optional border are combined into one image.

Photoshop Elements Canvas – Add space on any side of an image using [Image>Resize>Canvas Size]. Every image has a canvas the same size as the image until you change it. Resizing the canvas is a great way to add digital quilt borders or block sashing.

Digital Design Wall – Similar to the traditional quilting design wall, but you use a Photoshop Elements file to combine quilt blocks and play with color, placement, etc., so you can see what the whole project will look like before printing.

Project Sizing – We created all the blocks in this book as 8" square, 240 ppi resolution images, so you can resize them up to 12" x 12" 160 ppi resolution and print them on fabric just fine. You can easily make them smaller or larger via [Image>Resize>Image Size]. Note: the only exception is project 9, for which we used 300 ppi resolution so the calculated values would work properly.

Your computer disk space and memory may limit the file size and slow Photoshop Elements down. When insufficient RAM is available for image editing, Photoshop Elements uses a scratch disk file—temporary disk space used for storing data and performing computations. The drive you specify as the primary scratch disk should have free space equal to five times the size of the open image

file. If disk space is insufficient, then delete temporary files or remove other files from the hard disks.

To specify a scratch disk select [Edit>Preferences >Performance or Plugs-Ins & Scratch Disks] depending on your version.

The [File>New>Blank] file box displays the image size when you create a new file. The following sizes are for a new blank file with:
- **300 ppi resolution:**
  8" x 8" = 16.5 mb; 16" x 16" = 65 mb; 24" x 32" = 197.5 mb
- **240 ppi resolution:**
  8" x 8" = 10.5 mb; 16" x 16" = 42 mb; 24" x 32" = 110.4 mb

If you plan to create a large overall project and you will not be increasing the individual block sizes, we suggest reducing the resolution to 240 ppi for ALL the files including the block files to make designing faster.

Check out Chapter 6: Pixel Versatility for suggestions for different projects you can make from the same design.

Digital design step-by-step

1. Create a new blank design wall file.
Select [File>New Blank File]. Set the resolution to 240 ppi with a transparent background. Define the file size in multiples of 8" for the number of blocks in your design; for a 3 column x 4 row design, your file would be 24" wide by 32" high.

If you have an older computer with limited memory and disk space, create a smaller file in multiples of 4" for auditioning block placement. Resize the 8" blocks to 4" after adding them to the design wall, then print the individual 8" block files separately. For a 3 column x 4 row design, your file would be 12" wide x 16" high.

2. Move blocks onto the design wall file.
Open the block file. If the block is more than one layer, in the block file, go to [Select>All Layers] or press <CNTL a> or use the Marquee tool to select part of the block. Select [Edit>Copy Merged] or <SHIFT CTRL c>. Click on the design wall file and select [Edit>Paste]. Photoshop Elements merges all the layers in the block file into one layer in the design wall file.

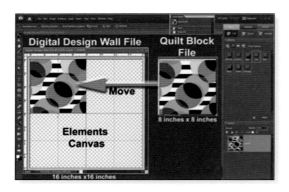

– *If the block is one layer,* click on the Move tool and drag the layer into the design wall file to the top left corner.

– *If the resolution is different between the block and the design wall files,* or you are working with a 4" based design wall, drag the block to resize it to fit in the upper left corner of the design wall grid.

Duplicate this layer and move it down or to the right, or add a different block. Many of the projects repeat one block, some rotating them like Bubbles. Bubbles, Checkerboard, Ocean Road, and the California Beauty projects combine several different blocks. The Bubbles, Checkerboard, and Ocean Road projects have step-by-step instructions for using a digital design wall.

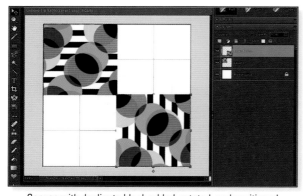

Canvas with duplicate block added, rotated, and positioned

Continue adding blocks or duplicating layers until the canvas is filled. In this example we copied the whole block onto the canvas and duplicated it. You could first copy one or more backgrounds onto the canvas, play with color, then Merge Visible to make one background layer. You could then add the foreground cookie shape layers on top of the background. We often save the background from one quilt and use it for other projects.

3. **Play with the design.**
Play until you are happy with the overall design and color. Get creative. Ask yourself what it would look like IF, and try the IF! You can easily undo something you don't like. Here are some suggestions:

– *Rotate or flip* some of the blocks to change the design. The previous illustration shows an example.

– *Play with color.* Make blocks lighter or darker or vary the hue slightly to subtly change them. Select [Enhance>Adjust Color>Color Variations or >Hue/ Saturation].

If you add your blocks to the design wall file in order by row from bottom to top, you can create a [New Adjustment Layer>Hue/Saturation] at the end of a middle row to change the master hue/saturation slightly. Notice that only the layers below the adjustment layer changed. You could reverse the order and put the top rows on the bottom of the layer stack, then lighten or grey them slightly.

Invert your design or part of it to its color wheel complement.

Refer to the Color Play section for detailed information and color examples.

– *Add cookie shapes on top of the blocks.* The Bubbles and Ocean Road projects create cookie shapes that span multiple blocks. Optionally change the opacity of the cookie shapes to make them more transparent.

When you have a project candidate, save the file as filename.psd. Continue playing and save several versions with different names until you have a masterpiece.

4. **Align the blocks.**
You need to check the block positions to make sure there is no blank space between them. Select [View>Print Size]. Move around the quilt top and nudge the blocks together if they are slightly off. Save the file as filename.psd.

5. **Decide how to print.**
If you plan to print the whole design on a large format printer or you want to reduce the size of your design to fit on one sheet (a miniature version), continue with step 6. If you want to add digital borders, continue with steps 7 and 8.

If your design wall file is larger than your printer size, skip ahead to steps 7 and 8.

6. Add optional digital borders.

Adding borders completes a wholecloth quilt printed as one piece of fabric.

a. Create a border on the canvas:
- Select [Image>Resize>Canvas Size].
- Turn on the Relative checkbox.
- For the border, enter double the border height and width. A width and height of 4" will create a 2" border around the top.
- For a border on two adjacent sides only, enter the full border height and width, then click on any corner arrow. The anchor picture changes, showing you where the border will occur.
- Click OK.
- Nudge any blocks into place along the border edges if needed.

b. Add a narrow inner border:
- With the Move tool, click on the top layer.
- Click on the new layer icon on top of the Layers palette to create the inner border layer.

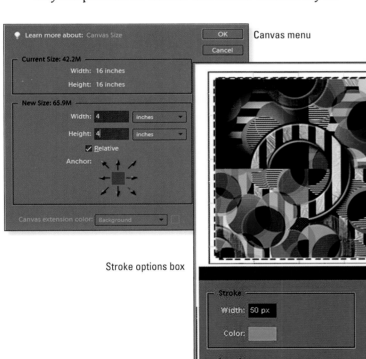

Canvas menu

Stroke options box

- Use the Eyedropper tool to click on a color for the inner border.
- To add the inner border, use the Marquee tool to draw a selection around your image.
- Select [Edit>Stroke].
- Enter 75 pixels. This determines the sashing width.
- Click on Location: Outside.
- Optionally change the color. Click OK.
- Undo and repeat if you want a thinner or thicker inner border.
- Press Esc to exit the Marquee tool.
- Optionally, change the color using Paint Bucket colors or patterns, or add layer styles such as bevels, drop shadows, inner or outer shadows, outer glows, patterns, or image effects.

c. Refine the outer border:
- Click on the design bottom transparent layer.
- Use the Paint Bucket to add a background color and apply Layer Styles patterns.
- Try another way to use a Paint Bucket pattern. Click on the Create Adjustment Layer icon in the Layers palette, and then select Pattern. The Pattern Fill menu appears and you can scale the pattern size.
- You could also define a pattern from your Digital Stash, and then apply it using a pattern adjustment layer. See the Color Play Paint Bucket section for details.

7. Save your file.

Save the file as filename.psd if you want to preserve the layers or as filename.jpg at the maximum–12 setting to flatten it.

8. Print on fabric.

Prepare the fabric for printing (see the Printing on Fabric section for details) and then select one of the following options to print:

– *Print the whole quilt in one piece if your printer width is large enough.* Print a small test strip on paper to check color and block alignment. Prepare the fabric, and then print. After printing on fabric, follow the manufacturer's instructions. Create a quilt sandwich as you would with any quilt. Quilt and bind.

You have several options when printing a design wall file where the narrowest top dimension is greater than your printer's width:

◦ Print each block file individually. If you saved each block before you pasted it to the design wall file and you did not change it in the design wall file, you can print each block the required number of times from the block files.

◦ Print each 8" block individually from the design wall file:

First, manually crop each block, one at a time, to 8" wide x 8" high, dragging the crop selection box exactly around the block edges.

Then, select [File>Print]. Under the page size pulldown menu, select Actual Size.

Optionally, print a test on paper to check color — 4" x 6" size is fine. Print on fabric.

Finally, undo the crop, and repeat (cropping, printing, and undo crop) until you have printed all the blocks.

– *Print the 8" blocks using your printer's multi-page printing option:*

◦ Most printers include a multi-page printing option, usually called multi-page or poster printing. Each printer is different. Look for it in your printer options.

◦ Set your margins so you print an 8" square on each sheet, or 8" by the printer roll height maximum if you use a roll of fabric.

◦ Print test pages on paper to check color and block alignment, then print on fabric.

9. **Follow the post-printing instructions.**

After printing on fabric, follow the manufacturer's instructions.

First, trim each square allowing a ¼" seam allowance as you would any pieced or appliquéd block.

Then, sew the blocks together to complete the top, using the project photo as a guide, and alternating or rotating blocks as shown.

Optionally, sew on a border.

Finally, create a quilt sandwich as you would with any quilt. Quilt and bind.

10. **Consider a final option.**

If you want to print the whole quilt top at once, take or e-mail your digital image to a company that will print your design on your choice of fabric. Commercial printers range in size from 24" to 60" so you have lots of options. If you aren't able to find a local printer who will print on fabric, try the Internet.

BUBBLES quilt (page 68) with two borders

PRINTING ON FABRIC

You can print your images at home using any ink-jet printer. Any natural-fiber fabric (e.g., cotton, silk, linen) will work if it is backed with paper to help it feed smoothly through the printer. To ensure that the results are at least as permanent as commercially-printed fabric, the fabric must be treated to ensure that the ink chemically bonds with the fabric.

Printers

There are many low-cost "ink-jet" or "bubble-jet" printers (or all-in-one copier/printer/scanners) available. Most print 8½" x 11" sheets and can manage 8½" widths by much longer lengths as well. We have used most of the name-brand printers successfully, but cannot vouch for other brands or new models that are just coming on the market.

The cost of wide-format printers has come way down in recent years, making them an attractive and reasonable alternative. For years, Gudny and Sandy have used different brands of printers that will print fabric that is up to 13" wide and up to 48" in length. Other models are available that can print fabric up to 17" wide. Professional-quality printers can print rolls or sheets of fabric from 24" to 60" wide, but require a big investment in money and space.

Inks

The inks in most inexpensive printers designed for home use are dye-based and penetrate into the fabric. They come in a single combination cartridge or separate cartridges for black and individual colors.

Many wide-format printers use pigment-based inks that stay on the surface of the fabric and are said to be archival (meaning they are less likely to damage the fabric and will last for decades). These printers may use as few as four ink cartridges (3 colors plus black) or as many as 8 (5 or 6 colors, one or more blacks).

Printer manufacturers state that you can print up to 650 8½" x 11" pages with one set of inks. BUT this assumes that only 5% of the area of the page is covered by images or text and that you are printing on a medium that absorbs relatively little ink. Since you will be printing on sheets of fabric that are densely covered by images and are more absorbent than paper, you will be able to print far fewer pages per set of ink cartridges, adding signifi-

cantly to the cost of digital quilting. Despite this, DO NOT USE BARGAIN INKS or refill company cartridges with second-party inks; they may not bond properly with the chemicals in treated fabric! And, no matter what printer you use, be sure to read the instructions! Boring but true.

Fabric

You can print on nearly any fabric, as long as it won't be exposed to water or sun. For permanent results, you must use a natural-fiber fabric (silk, cotton, or linen), treat the fabric so the ink will chemically bond with it (or buy it already treated), and complete the manufacturer's post-print-processing instructions. Different manufacturers recommend rinsing; heat-setting with an iron; washing out excess ink with detergent or special-purpose rinses; steaming; or spraying with fixative. Read the instructions!

It is usually best to print on plain white or off-white fabric with a fairly tight weave and a smooth surface; printers do not print "white" so the white parts of your image will be the same color as your background fabric. This can produce either interesting or unexpected results on colored or patterned fabric. Printing on textured, treated silk can produce especially beautiful results; the reflectivity of the different textures adds depth to your creation.

Remember, you are printing on fabric and need to consider the possibility of shrinkage. You can (and should) pre-shrink fabric that will be treated with Bubble Jet Set 2000® ink set. With purchased, pretreated fabric you can accomplish this step only after printing by rinsing in hot water, ironing when wet, or drying in a dryer—steps that may be a bit risky for different commercially available products. The best solution is to print a sample, cut it in half, try soaking it in hot water or using a dryer, and see if it fades or shrinks.

- **Purchase prepared fabric.**
  The easiest approach is to purchase paper-backed, treated fabric that is ready-to-use. Quilt and fabric stores sell packages of 8½" x 11", medium-weight cotton. Online sources offer steep discounts for bulk orders (e.g., 50 sheets at a time) and a variety of size and fabric choices (e.g., cotton sheeting, poplin, broadcloth, plain or patterned silk in different weights, and linen). Sheet sizes range

in width from 8½" x 11" to 13" x 19". Roll widths vary from 8½" to 60" and your choice of length. All of these products are colorfast and washable but the brightness of the printed images and hand of the fabric vary.

- **Prepare your own fabric.**

A less expensive and more flexible approach is to prepare fabric for printing yourself using Bubble Jet Set 2000, available in quilt and fabric stores and online. It extends your range of fabric types and dimensions and the results are nearly as good as with commercially-prepared products. One bottle can treat sixty 8½" x 11" sheets of cotton. The following is a quick review of how to use it:

  – *Wash the fabric in hot water* if it is not already prepared for dyeing (PFD) to preshrink and remove sizing. Dry it.

  – *Cut the treated fabric into strips* slightly wider than the size you want to print.

  – *Soak one or more strips* of fabric in Bubble Jet Set 2000 used full strength in a small plastic pan. Rub the liquid into each sheet until it is thoroughly saturated and let it soak for 5 minutes, then air dry.

  – *Just before using, trim the fabric* so it is ¼" smaller all around than the print size using a sharp rotary cutter.

  – Just before inserting into the printer, *firmly iron it to the shiny side* of freezer paper (grocery-store brand freezer, or heavier sheets sold for quilters which work better) cut to the exact print size. Be sure it is thoroughly bonded to the fabric.

Just before you print

The maximum width of fabric that you can print at a time is limited by the width of your printer's tray. The maximum length can be whatever you want (within reason). Within those limitations, you can print treated fabric of any dimensions as long as you set them up as custom sizes (in Page Setup) and then select the appropriate size for the current project when printing.

The specifics of printing vary among computers and printers, so check the following before printing:

1. **Define the printable area.**

Even printers said to be "borderless" may require that you set a print area slightly less than the maximum width; check print preview before you print to be sure all of your image is in the printable area (see the screen below).

2. **Check for optimal print quality.**

"Normal" for some printers and "best" or "fine" for others—the wrong setting may put either too little or too much ink on the fabric.

3. **Adjust the paper setting.**

Since few printer drivers offer a "fabric" option, find a close approximation (e.g., heavy matte paper, canvas, etc).

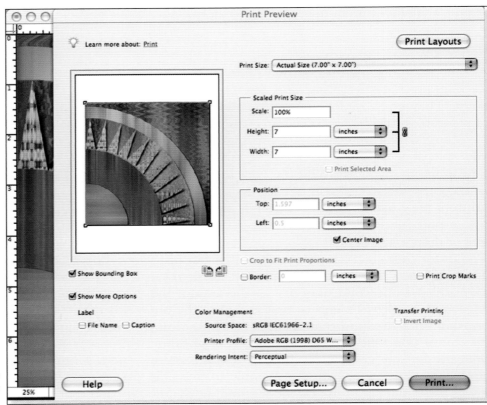

Print preview screen on a Mac using Photoshop Elements 4; the image will print with room to spare.

4. Set the paper thickness.

If available, move the manual setting to heavy/thick.

5. Verify the fabric orientation.

Check whether your printer requires fabric side up or down and then feed just one sheet at a time.

Be sure to remove bits of lint or threads from the surface of the fabric and carefully trim ALL stray threads around the edges.

Try the following remedies to solve problems:

– *If your print is too faint or light,* increase "gamma," contrast, and or saturation with image editing software and then try again. Or, use the "photo" paper option or "vivid" settings for your printer setup.

– *If the fabric won't feed,* insert sheets in one at a time. Iron them just before using. Round off the corners on the leading edges just a bit.

– *If the ink smears,* select a slower printing speed.

Post-print processing

After printing, wait until the fabric is completely dry and then peel the paper backing off. Most products require you to rinse the printed fabric to remove residual chemicals and excess dye that did not bond with the fabric. Always follow the manufacturer's instructions for the product you use. Then dry the fabric flat between towels or hang it to drip dry. If you aren't worried about shrinking, put it in the dryer for a few minutes.

A final option, particularly if you want to print the whole quilt top at once, is to take or e-mail your digital image to a company that will print your design on your choice of fabric. Commercial printers range in size from 24" to 60" so you have lots of options. If you aren't able to find a local printer who will print on fabric, try the Internet.

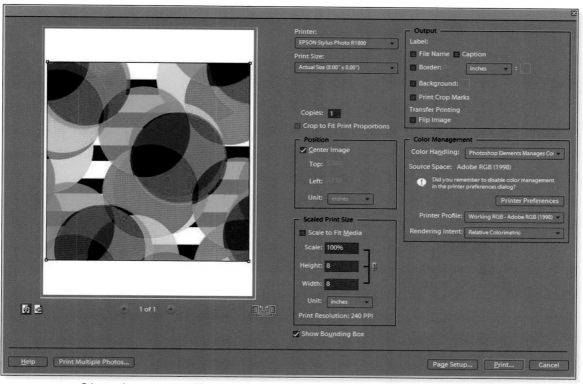

Print preview screen on a PC using Photoshop Elements 6; the edges of the image may not print.

Play and be creative. Try some projects. We include step-by-step instructions for nine projects that range in complexity from multiple copies of a simple block created with one cookie cutter shape (MOONLIT LEAVES) to traditional quilt blocks and innovative designs composed of multiple blocks and layers of shapes. We also suggest multiple ways to use your blocks.

Before you start the projects, we suggest you browse through chapters 1 through 4 and use them as a reference. If you need more information about something while you are working on a project, check the index.

Table: Project Materials List and Finishing Instructions

The following table shows the materials required to print and finish the project quilts.

Project	8" Blocks	8½" x 11" pretreated fabric sheets	Finished top size without border	Backing and Binding	Batting
1. MOONLIT LEAVES	3w x 5h	15	24" x 40"	1½ yards	28" x 44"
2. COASTAL PATH	2w x 6h	12	16" x 48"	1½ yards	20" x 52"
3. DOG BISCUITS	2w x 2h	4	16" x 16"	⅝ yard	20" x 20"
4. SQUARE COOKIES	4w x 4h	16	32" x 32"	1 yard	Crib size
5. BUBBLES	2w x 2h	4	16" x 16"	⅝ yard	20" x 20"
6. CHECKERBOARD	3w x 4h	12	24" x 32"	1 yard	28" x 36"
7. OCEAN ROAD	3w x 4h	12	24" x 32"	1 yard	28" x 36"
8. AUTUMN LEAVES	2w x 4h	8	16" x 32"	1 yard	20" x 36"
9. CALIFORNIA BEAUTY	4w x 5h	20	32" x 40"	1½ yards	36" x 44"
If you add a border, increase the yardage and batting sizes accordingly.					

Printing and finishing individual 8" blocks:

1. **To make one of the project quilts, optionally print a test on paper** to be sure that your printer prints colors the same way they look on the computer screen.
2. **Prepare the fabric, and then print the number of fabric sheets listed above** for your project. Note: if you need to print more than one block, refer to the project instructions and illustration.
3. **Treat the printed blocks** as recommended by the manufacturer.
4. **Trim each block** to 8½" square.
5. **Sew the blocks together** to complete the top, using the project photo as a guide, and alternating or rotating blocks as shown.
6. **Sew on an optional border.**

PROJECT 1: MOONLIT LEAVES

If you follow the steps required to create this simple, elegant, throw, you will have mastered the basics required to make any of the quilts in the book. For MOONLIT LEAVES, you need to create only two blocks in Photoshop Elements: one with silvery leaves on a black background, the other with black leaves on a silvery background. After printing 6 copies of each version and sewing them together, you will be ready to quilt this beauty inspired by moonlit nights in the tropics.

Leaf Ornament 1 cookie cutter

MOONLIT LEAVES, 24" x 40". Created and owned by Sandra Hart, 2008. Printed on Color Plus broadcloth with an HP Designjet z3100 printer.

Quilt Recipe

Cookie cutters:
   One 8" Leaf Ornament 1 cookie colored each of 2 ways
   One 8" foundation colored each of 2 ways
Finished size: 24" x 40"
Backing and binding: 1½ yards of a coordinating commercial fabric (I used black.)
Batting: Crib-quilt-sized piece of batting at least 28" x 44" (I used fusible.)
15 sheets of 8½" x 11" treated, paper-backed fabric

Instructions:

1. **Click on the Set Background Color icon** at the bottom of the tool bar. Click on black in the new screen, then click OK.
2. **Open a new 8" x 8" Blank file** with 240 ppi, RGB color, Background Color. [File> New>Blank File] or <CTRL n>

Create a background for the appliqué:

1. **Duplicate the black background layer** twice <CTRL j>. (See illustration.)

Need to Know

- Creating a new file with a colored background [Chapter 2 | THE BASICS]
- Cutting a cookie [Chapter 2 | THE BASICS]
- Applying and removing a layer style [Chapter 3 | FROSTING]
- Saving and printing a file [Chapter 2 |THE BASICS]

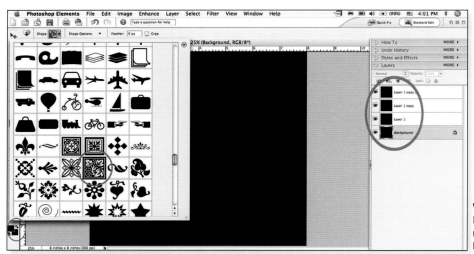

Workspace showing Layers palette, shapes menu, and foreground/ background colors

Hint

It is almost always better to work with a layer than the background.

Create the leaf appliqué:

1. **Select the top layer** by double clicking on its name in the Layers palette.
   For detailed instructions on cutting a shape with the Cookie Cutter, see Chapter 2: The Basics.
2. **Choose Layer Styles** from the Effects palette and Patterns from the drop-down menu on the right [Effects>Layer Styles>Patterns].
   For detailed instructions, see Chapter 3: Frosting.
3. **Select Ancient Stone** by double clicking on it and the layer will fill with Ancient Stone.
4. **Select the Cookie Cutter tool** from the Toolbar <q>.

- **Select Leaf Ornament 1** from the Ornament submenu.
- **Set Shape Options** to Fixed Size, 8" x 8".
- **Feather** = 0, **Crop** is off
- **Click on the workspace** to make the cookie cutter visible.

5. **Slide the Leaf cookie cutter around** until it is centered in the window. Accept it by pressing <ENTER>.
6. **The leaf appliqué will appear** on the background, a perfect appliqué that took two minutes!

Special Effects and Save:

1. If you want to gild the lily, **try adding a bevel** [Styles & Effects>Layer Styles>Bevels] to the top layer. I chose Simple Emboss, but you should try several options to find one that you like best. Double click on the Emboss icon to apply it.
2. **Save Version 1** with a distinctive name. [File>Save>Block1.psd]

Printing and finishing:

1. To make the 24" x 40" quilt shown, print 8 copies of Version 1 and 7 copies of Version 2.
2. After rinsing the printed blocks as recommended by the manufacturer, trim each to 8½" square.
3. Alternating version 1 and version 2, sew 3 rows that start with version 1 and 3 rows that start with version 2.
4. Sew the rows together, alternating rows that begin with version 1 with rows that begin with version 2.
5. Create a quilt sandwich as you would with any quilt and baste in preparation for quilting.
6. Several ways of quilting MOONLIT LEAVES come

Create Version 2:

1. **Select** the middle layer.
2. **Fill it** with Ancient Stone. [Effects>Layer Styles>Patterns>Ancient Stone]
3. **Select the top layer** and turn off the Layer Style [Layer>Layer Style>Clear Layer Style]. Voilà! You have reversed the coloration of the block.
4. **Put the same bevel on the top layer** (that is now black) that you did when it was colored Ancient Stone.
5. **Save Version 2** with a different name. Be sure to Save As or you will write over the first version. [File>Save As>Block2.psd]

Version 1   Version 2

to mind: outline the main parts of the leaf pattern with the appropriate color thread, and/or fill the black areas with a tight stipple so the moonlit areas stand out.

7. Bind as usual.

Variations on a Theme

If you don't want to print quite so many blocks, use a smaller number of blocks as a border for a table runner, placemats, tote bag, or vest. Create 4" x 4" blocks and print as many as you need, four to a page. See Chapter 6: Pixel Versatility for ideas. Another more complex version of this block is shown in project 8.

Play around with different combinations of solid colors and other types of layer styles (e.g., Complex, Image Effects, Photographic Effects) and see how far you can go with nothing more than the tools offered by Photoshop Elements and a single cookie cutter shape. See the examples on page 52.

Another option would be to use several similar cookie cutters and cut the shapes from photos of flowers, as in Gudny's HULA quilt, or out of pictures of dramatic California skies, as in Sandy's quilt. By arranging the different shapes carefully (and using only partial blocks on the edges), secondary patterns emerge. The CALIFORNIA SUNRISE quilt was printed on patterned silk, adding to the dramatic effects.

The next example was created by cutting the same shape (pattern 1) out of tree and sky photos, placing them on a background of the other photo, and then alternating the results.

The last example was created with the Leaf ornament cookie cutter applied to three leaves and a flower on a leaf background.

Examples using different background colors and layer style patterns

HULA, 32" x 32". A digital quilt created by Gudny Campbell in 2007 combining flower pictures and layer styles.

STACKED HULAS, 35" x 41". A digital quilt created by Gudny Campbell, 2007. Constructed by merging blocks cut with the Leaf Ornament cookie cutter into columns, then rotating and arranging them on a leafy background.

CALIFORNIA SUNRISES, 24" x 24". Created and owned by Sandra Hart, 2007. Printed on Silk Lines from Color Plus on a wide-format Epson printer.

PROJECT 2: COASTAL PATH

The project shows a great way to combine a dozen pictures from a special event or memorable trip into a one-of-a-kind wallhanging. This design is one of the many traditional quilt blocks you can make with Photoshop Elements Cookie Cutters and your own photos and Digital Stash. While it's a bit challenging to sew the curved seam in the Drunkards Path block, it's a snap to do it with the Quarter-circle cookie cutter.

Sandy chose 12 pictures of elephant seals on a California beach; for your own version you might choose: (1) flowers; (2) animals from a day at the zoo or bird watching; (3) scenes from a trip; or (4) a family holiday, such as Christmas. You could use the same or related pictures to create a Digital Stash for your background squares: (1) pictures of leaves from the same garden; (2) close-ups of animal hides from the zoo; (3) unsuccessful scenery pictures; or (4) Christmas paper or decorations.

COASTAL PATH, 21" x 53". Created and owned by Sandra Hart, 2008. Printed on Color Plus broadcloth with an HP Designjet z3100 printer.

Quarter-circle cookie cutter

Quilt Recipe

Cookie cutter: 8" Quarter-circle cookie
Finished size: 16" x 48" (21" x 53" with borders)
Border, backing, and binding: 1½ yards of commercial fabric
Batting: ⅔ yard of batting (from a 54" roll) or a crib-quilt-sized package pieced to get the needed length
12 sheets of 8½" x 11" treated, paper-backed fabric

Need to Know

- Applying a layer style
  [Chapter 3 | FROSTING]

New Skills

- Rotating a cookie before cutting it
  [Chapter 2 | RESIZE, ROTATE & FLIP]
- Creating a Digital Stash
  [Chapter 3 | DIGITAL STASH]

Get ready:

1. **Select focal images.** Find a group of pictures with a common theme and pleasing colors. Choose 12 that have a good focal image and save them in one folder.
2. **Create a Digital Stash.** Apply Photoshop Elements filters to each of the remaining pictures to create backgrounds for the quarter circles:
   - Open each photo.
   - Apply one or more filters until you create something wonderful.
   - Save the result with a unique name in a second folder.
   - Back up <CTRL z> to return to the original photo, or add additional filters until you have a nice selection to choose from.

   Sandy created many more options than she needed, and used this stash to make other quilts with a coastal theme (see examples and Variations on a Theme).

Original elephant seal pictures auditioned for the quilt

Examples of Sandy's COASTAL PATH Digital Stash

Create a background for the appliqué:

1. **Open a Digital Stash file** [File>Open] or <CTRL o>.
2. **Select the Crop tool** <c> and set **width and height** = 8 inches, **Resolution** = 240 ppi.
3. **Drag the Crop tool** across the image to select the part to use as a background and press <ENTER>.

Create the appliqué:

1. **Open a focus picture file** [File>Open] or <CTRL o>.
2. **Select the Cookie Cutter tool** from the toolbar <q> and set:
   - **Shape** = Quarter Circle
   - **Shape Options** = Defined Proportions. (You will "fussy cut" the quarter-circle to include the best part of the image and fine-tune its size later.)
   - **Feather** = 0
   - **Crop** = on
3. Cut the cookie by clicking on the image and sliding the Quarter-circle cookie cutter around until it is centered on the part of the picture you want to use. BEFORE YOU ACCEPT IT, specify how you want it to be oriented:
   - **Upper left:** Simply accept it.
   - **Upper right:** Type 90° into the Set Rotation window in the Cookie Cutter toolbar.
   - **Lower left:** Type -90° into the Set Rotation window in the Cookie Cutter toolbar.
   - **Lower right:** Type 180° into the Set Rotation window in the Cookie Cutter toolbar.
4. **Press** <ENTER> or select [✓].

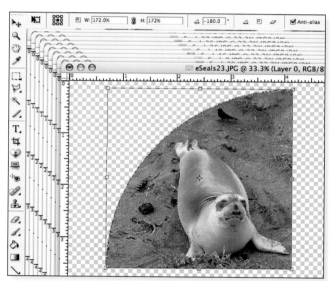

Setting up a quarter-circle that will fit in the upper left-hand corner

Setting up a quarter-circle that will fit in the lower right-hand circle

Resizing the quarter-circle

5. **Size the quarter-circle.** For a traditional Drunkard's Path, it would be 4" x 4" for an 8" background, but Sandy made hers larger (6") to show off the focal image. The quarter-circles can be the same for all blocks or you can vary them.
   - Select [Image>Size>Resize] or <CTRL ALT i>
   - **Width and Height** = 6" (or your choice)
   - **Resolution** = 240 ppi
   - **Scale Styles, Constrain Proportions, Resample Image** (Bicubic Smoother) = on

Create the block:

1. **Select** the Move tool <v>
2. **Drag** the quarter-circle into the background file with both files open and visible on the workspace.
3. **Position** it in the appropriate corner.

Special Effects and Merging:

1. **Add a bevel or shadow** to the quarter-circle to set it off from the background [Effects>Layer Styles>Bevels] if desired.
2. **Merge** the background and quarter-circle layers [Layer>Merge Visible] or <CTRL SHIFT e>
3. **Save this block** as a new JPEG file with a distinctive name [File>Save As] **and close** [File>Close] or press <CTRL w> without saving.

Printing and finishing:

1. **Repeat the process** 11 more times, choosing complementary backgrounds and focal images. Keep track of how many of each orientation you create if you have a specific layout in mind.
2. **Print the 12 blocks** and trim each to 8½" x 8½" after treating the fabric as recommended by the manufacturer.
3. **Arrange the blocks** until they create a pleasing layout.
4. **Sew the blocks** together in pairs and sew the 6 pairs together.
5. **Add a border** of coordinating fabric, if desired. I added 3" strips.
6. **Create a quilt sandwich** as you would with any quilt and baste in preparation for quilting.
7. **Quilting** around the quarter-circles and blocks is an obvious starting point. Then add motifs that complement the images in the quarter-circles.
8. **Bind** as usual.

NEW TWIST ON A DRUNKARDS PATH, 32" x 40". A digital quilt made and owned by Sandra Hart, 2008.

Variations on a Theme

Three versions of Drunkards Path-type quilts are shown on these pages. Sandy created the first with many copies of the same two 4" blocks, alternating mirror images of a colored and white piece of Digital Stash. Black, red, and blue versions were created using [Enhance>Adjust Color>Color Variations]. She created the unsteady path by cutting several appliqués using the Nature: River 1 shape from a layer filled with plain black and arranging them across the completed top.

Coastal Ovals, 22½" x 36". Created and owned by Sandra Hart, 2008. Printed on cotton poplin by Color Plus on an HP Deskjet z3100.

Coastal Ovals was created from a large Digital Stash based on photographs of California beach scenes, skies, flora, and fauna. Each 4½" block has two overlapping "backgrounds" exposing a pointed oval shape in the middle. Tiny ½" squares cut from the same stash were layered over half of the intersections to create little 4-patches. The quilting depicts California coastal motifs.

Trip to Mt. Shasta was a joint effort with Sandy's six-year old grandson, Caleb; after learning how to make a Digital Stash, Caleb took dozens of pictures of interesting colors and textures on a trip to Mt. Shasta and Sandy created two versions of the quilt using his Digital Stash (one with and one without the original snapshots). Unlike a traditional Drunkards Path, the sizes of the quarter-circle appliqués stacked on the background squares were varied and rotated to create lively quilts.

Trip to Mt Shasta, 24" x 36". Created by Sandra Hart in 2007. Printed on cotton poplin by Color Plus on an HP Deskjet z3100.

PROJECT 3: DOG BISCUITS

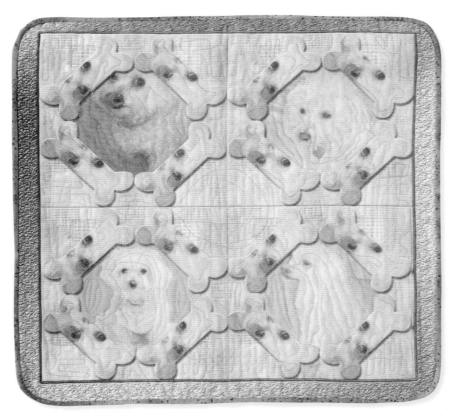

The project steps through cutting and rotating a symmetrical cookie shape out of one or more pictures, and arranging them in combination with other pictures to create a themed quilt. The project uses cute dog pictures and a dog-themed cookie shape. Variations on a theme suggests other possibilities if you are not a "dog person."

DOG BISCUITS, 20" x 20", by Gudny Campbell, 2008. Photos of my granddaughter's dog Fifi were used.

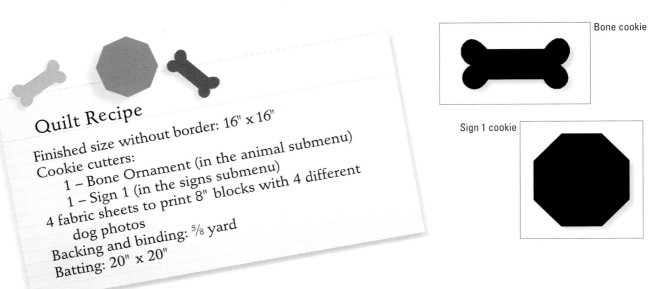

Bone cookie

Sign 1 cookie

Quilt Recipe

Finished size without border: 16" x 16"
Cookie cutters:
    1 – Bone Ornament (in the animal submenu)
    1 – Sign 1 (in the signs submenu)
4 fabric sheets to print 8" blocks with 4 different
    dog photos
Backing and binding: ⅝ yard
Batting: 20" x 20"

Need to Know

- Matching a photo subject and cookie theme
- Rotating a layer
  [Chapter 2 | RESIZE, ROTATE & FLIP]
- Applying layer styles
  [Chapter 3 | FROSTING]

Instructions:

1. **Create the block file and set preferences.**
   - Select [File>New>Blank File], 8" wide, 8" high, 240 ppi resolution, white background. Click on OK.
   - Select [Edit>Preferences>Grid], gridlines every 4", 2 subdivisions. Click OK.
   - Select [View>Grid] on and [Snap To Grid] on.
   - Select [Window>Images>Cascade].

2. **Create the quilt block background using layer styles.**
   - Select [Layer Styles–Complex>White grid on orange]. Rest the cursor on a style to see its name. Double click.

     You will get the message, "Styles can only be applied to layers. Do you want to make this background a layer?" Click on OK. Rename the layer if desired, then click OK again.
   - Select [Layer Styles–Image Effects>Fog]. Double click. Note: You could have used an image or any other layer style to create a background.

3. **Open the image file and create the bone cookie.**
   - Open a suitable image [File>Open] and resize it [Image>Resize>Image Size] to at least 6" wide and 6" high, 240 ppi resolution.
   - Select the Bone Cookie in the Animals category. On the Cookie Cutter Options bar, click [crop ON].

- Click on workspace.
- In Shape Options set [Defined Proportions ON].
- Move the cookie around until you like what is inside the bone. This is like fussy cutting. Press enter.
- With both files open and visible in the workspace, drag the bone cookie to the quilt block file. Close the image file without saving.

4. **Add layer styles.**
   Select Layer Styles to enhance the bone. We selected two: (Bevels–Simple Emboss and Drop Shadows–Low.) Double click to apply.

5. **Free rotate the bone cookie layer.**
   - With the Move tool (v) and bone cookie layer selected, move the cursor until it is just OUTSIDE the boundary box that appears around the cookie and click.
   - Gradually rotate the cookie around until the boundary box is a diamond shape, or you can type "45" into the Set Rotate box in the Free Transform Options bar, which appears at the top of the workspace (circled in red in the picture of the workspace).
   - When you are satisfied, press <ENTER>.

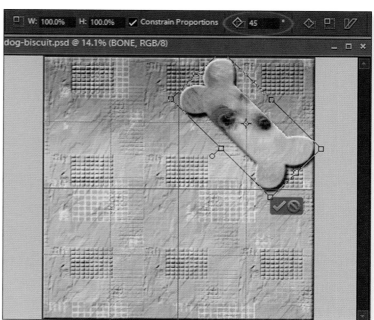

Free Rotate and Resize bone cookie

6. **Resize the bone cookie layer.**

   Click ON the bounding box and resize the cookie to fit in the upper left quarter and line it up with the grid. You can make the whole thing smaller or larger. When you are satisfied, press Enter or click on the green checkmark (V. 5, 6 & 7).

7. **Duplicate the bone cookie layer.**
   - Click on the bone layer and press <CTRL j> three times.
   - With the Move tool selected <v>, move each of the new layers to the other corners.

8. **Rotate layers to form a frame.**

   Click on each of the new bone cookies, then select [Image>Rotate>Rotate Layer 90° right (or left)] to fit. (See the picture of the block.)

9. **Create the octagon (sign 1) cookie.**
   - Select [File>Open] to open the center image file.
   - Select [Image>Resize>Image Resize] to resize to at least 7" wide and 7" high, 240 ppi resolution.
   - Select the Sign 1 Cookie from the Signs sub-menu.
   - On the cookie cutter options bar, click crop ON. Set Shape Options to Fixed Size 6" wide, 6" high.
   - Move the cookie around until you like what is inside the octagon. Press [ENTER].
   - Drag the octagon cookie shape to the block file and on the Layers palette, drag it below all the bones layers.
   - Close the image file without saving, to preserve the original image. [File>Close>don't save] <CTRL w>

10. **Save your block as a PSD.**
   - Now that your first block is complete, repeat steps 9 and 10 three more times to create the 4 blocks with different octagon inserts.
   - Save your block with a different file name each time.
   - Print the blocks on fabric, sew together, and add an optional border.
   - Sandwich, quilt, and bind, or make into a pillow.

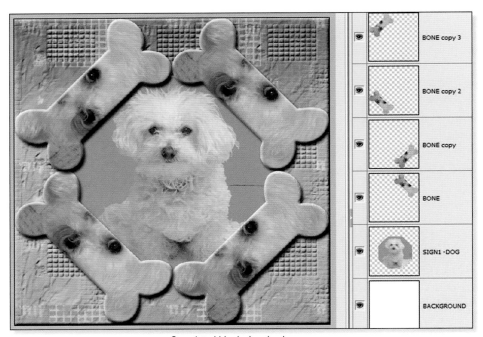

Completed block showing layers

Variations on a Theme

Digital image. Gudny copied and free rotated the Ribbon 1 cookie four times and added an oval photo of a granddaughter with her ribbons.

Digital block. Created by copying and rotating solid and outlined hearts cut from flower photos.

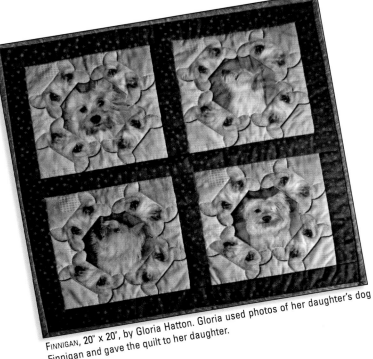

Finnigan, 20" x 20", by Gloria Hatton. Gloria used photos of her daughter's dog Finnigan and gave the quilt to her daughter.

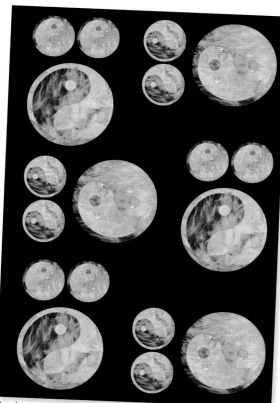

Sandy created this digital image of six blocks with two small Yin Yang cookies and one large one. Each block is rotated slightly differently.

PROJECT 4: SQUARE COOKIES

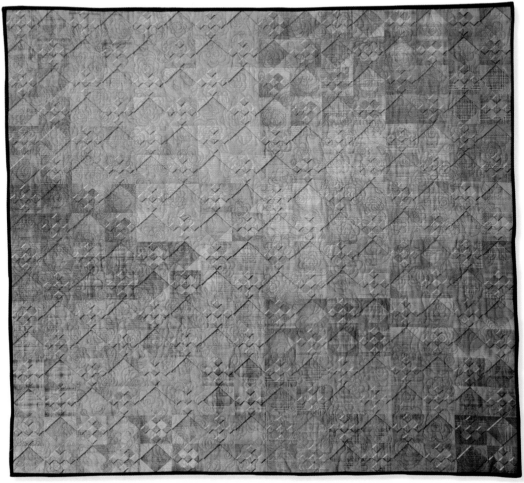

SQUARE COOKIES, 48" x 48". Created and owned by Sandra Hart, 2008.
Printed on cotton broadcloth by Color Plus on an HP Designjet z3100.

This is a traditional "Rob Peter to Pay Paul" type of quilt; the arrangement of dark and light fabrics is reversed in alternate blocks. Because Sandy wanted to use all of her plaid Digital Stash, she created lots of relatively small 3" blocks combined into 6" block sets. However, the instructions are given for 4" blocks and 8" block sets, resulting in a 32" finished quilt.

To speed constructions, consider making your blocks twice as large, printing one block set per sheet of fabric. Depending on the colors and textures you use and the numbers of block sets you print, it would make a beautiful table topper, baby quilt, or wallhanging or use a few blocks to decorate the edges of placemats or a vest.

Diamond and Ornament 4
Cookie Cutters used

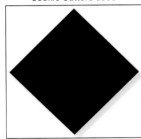

Quilt Recipe

Cookie cutters:
   Diamond (in shapes submenu), Ornament 4
   (in ornament submenu)
Finished size: 32" x 32"
Backing and binding: 1 yard of a coordinating
   commercial fabric for backing and binding.
   A border could be added as well.
Batting: crib-quilt-sized piece
16 sheets of 8½" x 11", treated, paper-backed fabric

Need to Know

- The Basics [Chapter 2]
- Creating a Digital Stash [Chapter 3 | DIGITAL STASH]
- Adding layer styles [Chapter 3 | FROSTING]
- Merging layers [Chapter 2 | MORE ABOUT LAYERS]

New Skills

- Combining four smaller blocks into one larger block

What to do:

Each block set consists of four 4" background squares, topped with four 4" diamonds. Two of the blocks have additional tipped 9-patches on top, as shown below.

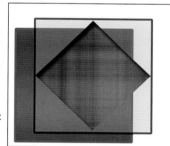

Layers for block files:
version 1, right;
version 2, below

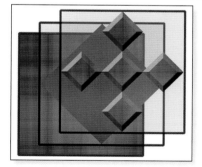

Get ready:

1. **Create a Digital Stash from photos that have complementary colors.** Sandy used two filters for each photo (Offset to create plaids and Motion Blur to create a subtle "solid"; see the Digital Stash section for details). See the following examples of the Plaid and Blur stashes Sandy used for this quilt.

2. **Open two new 4" x 4", 240 ppi, RGB files with a white background** [File>New>Blank file] or <Ctrl n>. Turn the backgrounds off.

3. **Open two files from your Digital Stash.** Sandy used a plaid and a blur from the same photo. Arrange the four open files on the desktop as shown.

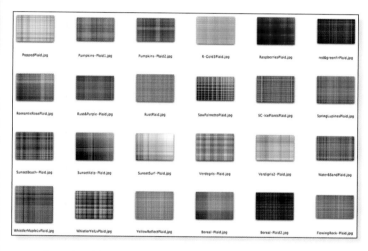

Examples of Digital Stash files created for the SQUARE COOKIES quilt: Plaids, above; Blurs, below

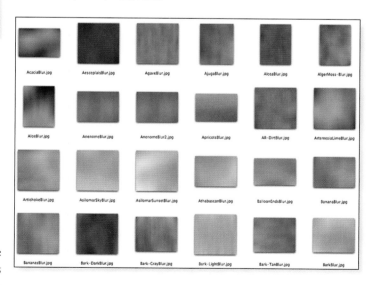

Create backgrounds:

1. **Select the Crop tool** <c>. Enter 4" width, 4" height, 240 ppi resolution in the options bar.

2. **Click on each Digital Stash file.**

3. **Select the best part** of each image with the Crop tool, <ENTER>.

4. **Select the Move tool** <v> and click on one square, dragging it into each block file using the mouse. When you release the button on the mouse, a copy of that layer will appear in the destination file.

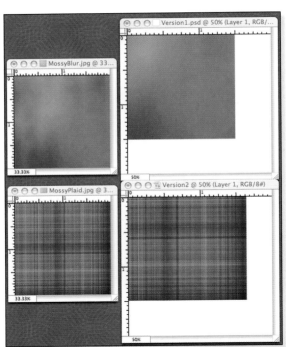

Cropped Digital Stash files being moved into Version 1 and 2 block files

Create the appliqués:

1. **Select the Cookie Cutter** <q>:
   • **Shape** = Diamond (be sure to choose the right one)
   • **Shape Options** = Fixed size 4" x 4", **Feather** = 0, **Crop** = off

2. **Return to the Digital Stash files** and cut a 2" diamond from each.

3. **Select the Move tool** <v> and drag the diamonds into the opposite block files.

4. **Select the Cookie Cutter** again <q>:
   • **Shape** = Ornament 4
   • **Shape Options** = Fixed size, 4" x 4", **Feather** = 0, **Crop** = off

5. **Return to one of the Digital Stash files** and cut the tipped 9-patch from the diamond.

6. **Select the Move tool** <v> and drag the tipped 9-patch to the block file with the opposite diamond.

7. **Arrange the layers** so they are neatly lined up in the block files, <ENTER>.

8. **Close the Digital Stash files** without saving.

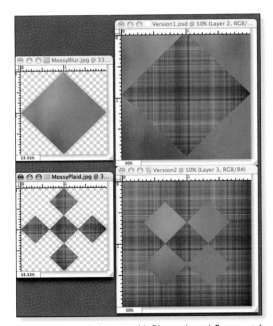

Additional layers being cut with Diamonds and Ornament 4 cookie cutters and moved to Block files

Frosting:

Add bevels or shadows to the edges of some or all of the components. We used a Reverse Shadow for the plaid diamonds and a Simple Sharp Inner Bevel for the tipped 9-patch. Remember what you did because you may want to repeat it for the next block.

Create a Block Set:

A block set is a group of four blocks merged to create a larger block.

1. Merge the square, diamond, and tipped 9-patch Layers. [Layer>Merge visible] or <CTRL shift e>.

2. Open a 8" x 8" Block Set file (240 ppi, RGB, white background) [File>New>Blank file] or <CRTL n>.

3. With 2/1 grid selected [Edit> Preferences>Grid] and snap to grid on [View>Snap To], **drag Version 1 and Version 2 into the Block Set file.**

4. Duplicate each block. Select [Layer> Duplicate Layer] or press <CTRL j>.

5. Arrange the four blocks as shown. Merge Visible layers as in #1 and save as a JPEG. Select [File>Save As>new name] or press <CTRL shift s>.

6. Return to the block files, and delete the layers containing the block you just made. The block files are ready to be used again to make another block with a new pair of Digital Stash files.

Printing and finishing:

1. **Print the Block sets,** one to a page on 8½" x 11" treated fabric.

2. After treating the printed blocks as recommended by the manufacturer, **trim** to 8½" x 8½".

3. **Sew** the rows and then columns together and add a border, if desired.

4. **Create a quilt sandwich** as you would with any quilt and baste in preparation for quilting.

5. **Quilt in the ditch** around the squares, diamonds, and tipped 9-patch.

6. **Bind** as usual.

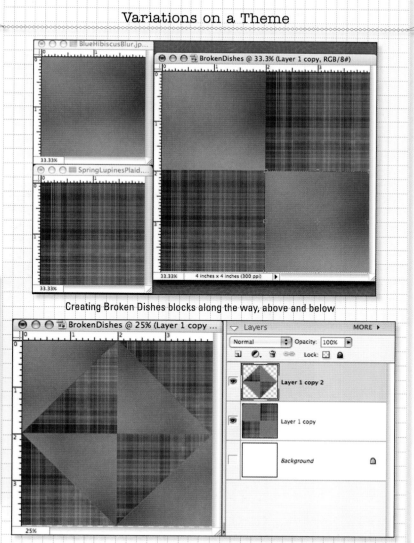

Variations on a Theme

Creating Broken Dishes blocks along the way, above and below

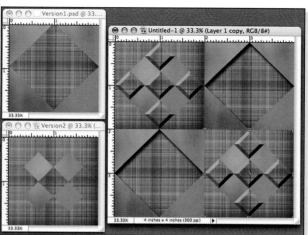

Block files frosted with bevels and shadows, moved into the Block Set file

Variations on a Theme

1. Make two quilts at the same time.

While the two Digital Stash files are open, move the same pairs of "fabric" into a third 8" x 8" Block file. Duplicate each one and arrange them as shown in Variations on a Theme on page 65. Merge the four layers and cut an 8" diamond from the top layer. Rotate the diamond layer 90° right [Image>Rotate>Layer 90 Right]. Voilà! You have created a Broken Dishes block in a minute or two. If you make and save these blocks as you make the project-quilt blocks, you will be ready to make a second quilt.

Version 1 and Version 2 blocks. Each block starts with an 8" square, with an 8" diamond on top, and a 4" square on top of that. Alternating digital stash choices, print as many blocks as you need to make a very quick and easy gift.

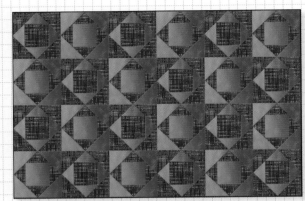

A simple quilt created from alternating blocks created with only two pieces of Digital Stash

4. Start with Painted Layers or Digital Stash

Try creating it from layers filled with solid colors. This is even easier—open a 4" x 4" block with a black background. Cut a 4" diamond. Then fill the triangles that remain around the edges with whatever color you wish using the Paint Bucket <k> as described in the COLOR PLAY section. Add a second square on top if you wish.

For a more interesting quilt, print each set of four blocks with a different combination of black and a primary color (for a young child) or white and pastels (for a baby), again using the Paint Bucket and Layer Styles on the colored pieces in the pastel version. [Styles & Effects>Inner Shadows>High].

JUST ROSES. A baby quilt made from the first two layers of blocks (that were cut from images that started with a rose), saved before adding the tipped 9-patch block.

2. Make three quilts at the same time.

If you are even more ambitious, save some or all of the blocks without the additional tipped 9-patch layer. Add different types of frosting (in the sample, Simple Inner Bevel was added to all of the plaid pieces and an Inner Ridge Bevel was placed around each block set before it was arranged on a black background.

3. Repeat the same Block set.

Using just two pieces of Digital Stash, make 3-Layer

Two multicolor digital quilts cut from painted layers filled with (above) brights and black, and (right) pastels and white

Variations on a Theme

5. Add interesting images on top.

Go a little further and add a variety of kid-friendly shapes in contrasting colors to painted layers in the top photo and jazz them up by adding an inner shadow to the fish to give the appearance of reverse appliqué; filling the butterfly with dazzling colors [Effects>Layer Styles>Patterns>Angled Spectrum]; turning the Rabbit silhouette into a shiny outline [Effects>Layer Styles>Wow Neon>Neon Purple Off]; or adding a beveled edge to the elephant [Effects>Layer Styles>Bevels Simple Sharp].

Instead of adding animal shapes to the basic block, try more sophisticated cookie cutters, such as a stylized rose and leaf. Add the Rose and Magenta Layer Style to the black sections and recolor the pink sections to complement them using the Paint Bucket. Another option is to create a basic block from your stash (Sandy applied filters to a photo of broccoli), adding a bevel, and then superimposing pictures of your own flowers cut with the Flower 23 Cookie Cutter.

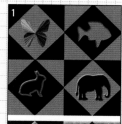
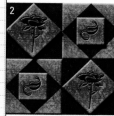
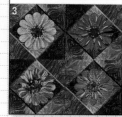

Two-color blocks cut from: (1) painted layers decorated with cookies cut from solid colors jazzed up with layer styles; (2) plain and frosted layers; and (3) Digital Stash decorated with flower photos

Additional Ideas

a. Add the Complex/Paint Brush Stroke and Scalloped-edge Bevels to every layer.

b. Create basic blocks with Digital Stash made from leaf and sky photos. Cut two of the diamonds from flower photos.

c. Color all pieces with Complex/Sunset, then add Complex/White Grid on Orange Layer Style, Simple Inner Bevel, and High Drop Shadow to half of them.

d. Transform half of the pieces with the Plum Glass Buttons Layer Style.

e. Color half of the pieces magenta, then add a Complex/Rose Impressions Layer Style.

f. Color all of the pieces magenta, then add a Complex/White Grid on Orange Layer Style to half.

g. Transform half of the pieces with the Complex/Red with Gradient Layer Style.

h. Transform half of the pieces with the Complex/Rainbow Layer Style.

i. Transform half of the pieces with the Patterns/Angled Spectrum Layer Style.

Any one of these sets of blocks could be printed several times and combined to create a wallhanging, table topper, throw, etc.

Hint

To make transforming layers easier, try merging all of the layers that are one color into one layer, and merge the rest into a second. Select the layers by clicking on the layer name one at a time with the mouse while holding down the Control key with your left hand. When all of them have been selected, merge layers (press <CTRL e>).

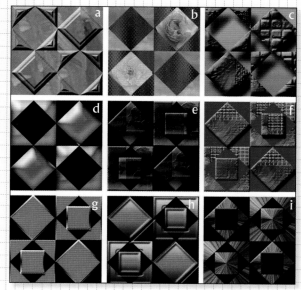

More ideas: Mix layer styles, photos, and Digital Stash to create different looks for the basic block.

Project 5: Bubbles

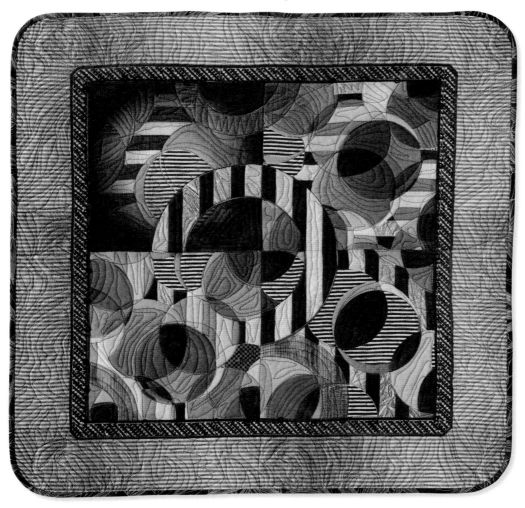

Bubbles is an abstract design contrasting brightly colored "bubbles" with graphic black-and-white stripes in the background. The stripes patterns and block background were created with Halftone filters in the block file and then arranged in a Digital Design Wall file. Circle Frame cookie shapes were arranged on top and colored with Paint Bucket patterns.

Bubbles, 23" x 23". Created and owned by Gudny Campbell, 2008.

Circle Frame
cookie cutter

Quilt Recipe

Cookie cutter: Circle Frame

Finished size without border: 16" x 16"

Backing and binding: ⅝ yard

Batting: 20" x 20"

Border: ⅓ yard

4 sheets of 8½" x 11" treated, paper-backed fabric

Need to Know

The Basics [Chapter 2 | BASICS]

New Skills:

- Using filters to create halftones
  [Chapter 3 | DIGITAL STASH]
- Defining and using Paint Bucket patterns
  [Chapter 3 | COLOR PLAY]
- Creating shading and transparency
  [Chapter 3 | COLOR PLAY]
- Arranging on a Digital Design Wall
  [Chapter 4 | DESIGNING AND PRINTING]

Instructions:

Overview:

- **In steps 1 – 3** you open a very small blank file, and create and define a stripes pattern.
- **In steps 4 – 7** you create the quilt block using the Halftone filter to create the pattern and increase the block file size to 8".
- **In steps 8 – 10** you create the design wall file, and move quilt blocks onto it from the block file.
- **In steps 11 – 14** you work in the design wall file, placing cookie circle shapes on top of the quilt blocks, adding layer styles and playing with color and pattern.

1. Create the block file.

Select [File>New>Blank File] or <CTRL n>, 1" x 1" (a very small file), 300 ppi resolution and a white background.

2. Set the default colors to black and white.

- On the Set Foreground Color box, set the default colors to black and white (Note: the quick way to do this is to press <d>). DO NOT SKIP THIS STEP!
- With the Paint Bucket tool <k>, color the layer white.

3. Define narrow stripes and Paint Bucket pattern.

- From the top pull-down menu, select

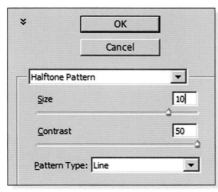
Halftone Pattern box settings

[Filter>Sketch>Halftone Pattern]. Click on Pattern Type and set **Size** = 10, **Contrast** = 50, **Pattern type** = Line. Click OK or press <ENTER>. Besides the line there are also circle and dot options. Some other time, select them and play.

- Select [Edit>Define Pattern], name it *stripes-narrow* and click OK or press <ENTER>.
- Undo or press <CTRL z> once to deselect the halftone, reverting to the white background.

For more information on using Paint Bucket patterns see Chapter 3: COLOR PLAY/ Paint Bucket.

4. Create the stripes background.

- From the top pull-down menu, select [Filter>Sketch>Halftone Pattern] again to create wider stripes.
  Size = 12,
  Contrast = 50,
  Pattern type = line. Click OK or <ENTER>.
- Duplicate this stripes layer. <CTRL j>

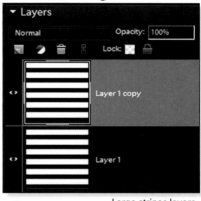
Large stripes layers

5. Create the bubbles layer.

- Click on the top stripes layer, and from the top pull-down menu select [Filter>Pixelate>Color Halftone]. Enter the following settings using the mouse or tabs to move from one box to the next:
  Max Radius = 127
  Channel 1 = 127
  Channel 2 = 220
  Channel 3 = 200
  Channel 4 = 45
  Click OK.
- Double click on the layer title and change it to 1/2 tone 127 – 127 220 200 45. Naming the layer title is helpful, and this

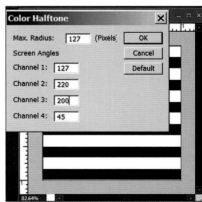
Color Halftone box settings

is a shorthand way to document the filter and settings you used in case you want to use them again.

6. **Add a striped background to the bubbles layer.**
   - Click on the Magic Wand tool <w> and click on the white background of the bubbles layer. On the options bar, set the Tolerance to 15 and Contiguous off. Press the delete key. The stripes layer below shows and becomes the background.
   - Press ESC. Do not merge the layers.

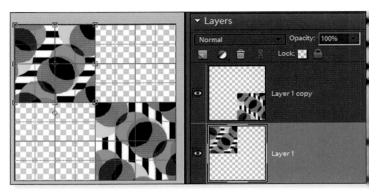

Design Wall file with first block duplicated and rotated (grid is red)

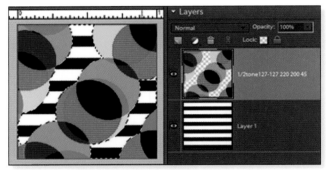

After deleted white color with Magic Wand

7. **Increase the quilt block size to 8".**
   - From the top pull-down menu, select [Image>Resize>Image Size] or select <CTRL SHIFT i> and resize the block size to 8" square with 240 ppi. Set Constrain Proportions and Resam-ple Image on and select Bicubic Smoother.
   - Select [File>Save As] to save your block as file-name.psd. Do NOT save as a JPEG file.

8. **Create a Digital Design Wall file, then drag and arrange the first block on it.**
   - Select [File>New>Blank File]:
     Width = 16 inches
     Height = 16 inches
     Resolution = 240 ppi
     Background contents = transparent
   - Click on the open quilt block file that you saved in step 7.
   - Press <CTRL a>, and then select [Edit>Copy Merged] or <CTRL shift c>. Click on the new 16" design wall file, then select [Edit>Paste] <CTRL v>. Move the bubbles block layer to the top left. <ENTER>.
   - Duplicate the layer <CTRL j>, and rotate it 90° to the left [Image>Rotate>Layer 90° left].
   - Move it to the bottom right.

9. **Create a second Bubbles quilt block.**
   - Click on the open block file you just saved in step 7.
   - Duplicate the top bubbles layer <CTRL j>.
   - Rotate the new top copy layer left 90°. Set the new layer opacity to 65%, using the slider in the upper right corner of the Layers palette (see picture).
   - You should be able to see both half tone layers (the colored bubbles), the striped bottom layer, and all sorts of new shadows and transparencies.
   - Again, do not merge the layers.
   - Select [File>Save As PSD] to save your file again.

10. **Move the second Bubbles quilt block to the design wall file.**
    - Press <CTRL a> and then select [Edit>Copy Merged].
    - Click on the design wall file, then select [Edit>Paste].
    - Move the layer to the top right.
    - Duplicate the layer <CTRL j>.
    - Rotate the layer right 90° [Image>Rotate>Layer 90° Right], and move it to the bottom left.
    You should have 4 blocks in the design wall file.

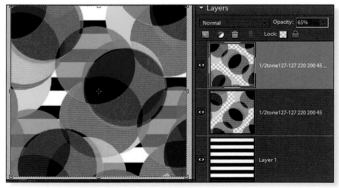

Block file showing second Bubbles block and layers

11. **Add the center Circle Frame cookie shape.**
    - In the block file, duplicate the stripes layer <j>. Hide all the layers except the bottom stripes layer.
    - Click on the bottom stripes layer.
    - Select [Image>Rotate>Layer 90° Left].
    - Click on the Cookie Cutter tool and select the Circle Frame cookie from the shapes submenu. Set **crop** = off and fixed size to 8" by 8", then cut the circle from the rotated layer.
    - Save the block file as a PSD.

12. **Place the circle cookie in the design wall file.**
    - Drag the circle layer into the design wall file.
    - In the design wall file, make the circle slightly larger, and arrange it so it is off-center and the vertical stripes are offset on the right.
    - Click on the bottom left layer, then select [Layer>Arrange>Bring to Front]. The circle will be behind this layer and in front of the others.
    - Add layer styles such as Bevel and Drop Shadow to the circle if desired. Refer to the Frosting section for more information.

13. **Add shadow layer styles.**
    Top Left Layer
    Layer Style>Image Effects>
    Circular Vignette
    Layer Style>Photographic Effects>Negative
    Top Right Layer
    Layer Style>Image Effects>
    Color Fade Horizontal
    Layer Style>Image Effects>Color Burn
    Bottom Left Layer
    Layer Style>Image Effects>
    Color Fade Vertical
    Lower Right Layer
    Layer Style>Image Effects>Colorful Center
    Layer Style>Image Effects>Color Burn
    Layer Style>Image Effects>
    Color Fade Horizontal

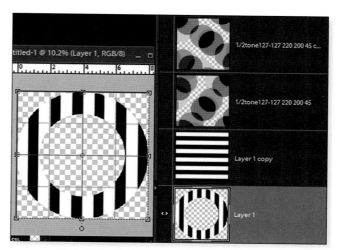

Block file showing layers and circle cookie shape

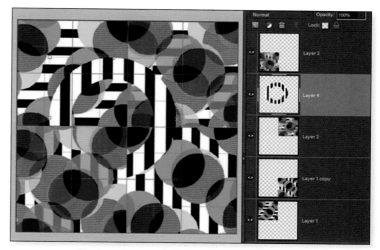

Blocks and center circle arranged on design wall

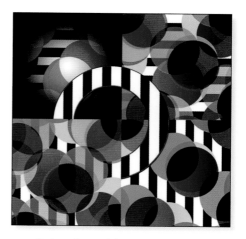

Project after applying shadow effects

14. **Play with color and pattern.**
    - Look at Variations on a Theme to see a few possibilities that we created, and then create some of your own.
    - Use the Paint Bucket foreground color to change the template's colors and patterns.
    - Click on a layer, then click on the Paint Bucket tool and select pattern from options bar. You should see the stripe pattern you created on the bottom.
    - Set tolerance to around 20. Set Contiguous on or off depending on what you want to color. Click on some of the colors to change them to stripes. With Contiguous on you can change individual stripes. Repeat coloring until you are satisfied.
    - Optionally, create and define a light-colored pattern to replace the white, or switch to foreground mode and change other colors.
    - Repeat for all the layers.
    - If you don't want to keep the stripe pattern, when you are done coloring, delete it in the pattern menu.

15. **Optional: Add more circle frames.**
    Create several circle frames from your Digital Stash or photo files and place them on top of the design. The project uses 3 partial circle frames on the bottom and top. Create the full circle frames. Move them off the edge or below the left bottom layer. Set the circle frame layer opacity to around 75%.

16. **Finishing**
    Save the design wall file as filename.psd if you want to change it later. Follow steps 4 through 8 in Chapter 4, the Digital Design Wall section, to complete and print on fabric, then follow the instructions for your size quilt in the Pixel Versatility section. If you plan to print as one piece (on a large format printer or reduced size), consider adding a digital border.

Variations on a Theme

Right: Digital quilt by Gudny Campbell. She combined various size blocks and created a border by copying and enlarging the top.

Digital quilt by Gudny Campbell. She played with color halftone settings, then stretched one 8" block to make it 16" square, colored it with patterns, and added a mosaic filter border.

Digital quilt by Sandy Hart. She added circles cut from photos of knitted rainbows.

Right: Digital quilt – variation of quilt above right by Gudny Campbell. She defined and used patterns from photos of flowers and butterflies.

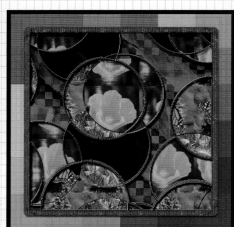

PROJECT 6: CHECKERBOARD

Use a photo with two main colors, and different cookie cutters alone or in combination to create layered checkerboard effects. The project creates four quilt blocks, then duplicates, rotates, and modifies their color to add richness and complexity. You can stop with one block, create two, or create a mix of all the blocks.

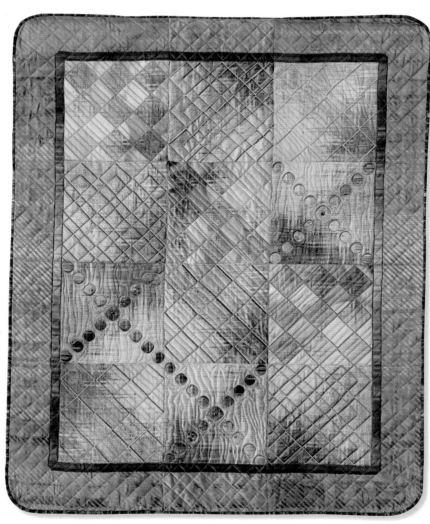

CHECKERBOARD, 32" x 40", by Gudny Campbell, 2009. A photo of a blue and yellow iris was used.

Quilt Recipe

Cookie cutters:
    Tiles 2, 3, 4 (in the Tiles submenu),
    Square (in the Shapes submenu)
Finished size without borders: 24" x 32"
Border (optional): ½ yard
Backing and binding: 1 yard without border;
    1½ yards with border
Batting size: 28" x 36" without the border,
    34" x 42" if a border is added
12 sheets, 8½" x 11" treated, paper-backed
    fabric for the top

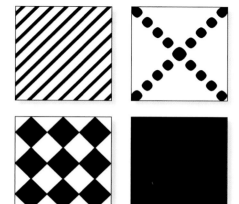

Cookie cutters used in the project:
Tile 2, Tile 3, Tile 4, Square

> ## Need to Know
> - [Chapter 2 | MORE ABOUT PHOTOS]
> - [Chapter 3 | COLOR PLAY]
> - [Chapter 4 | DIGITAL DESIGN WALL]
>
> ## New Skills
> - Stroke – to outline cookies

Instructions:

1. Create the design wall file and set preferences.

You will work with two files: (1) your image saved as a PSD in which you will create the four quilt blocks, and (2) a Digital Design wall file.

Follow step 1 in Chapter 4: Digital Design Wall section to create a design wall file, setting the resolution to 240 ppi. Project file size is 24" wide by 32" high. Change the size as desired.

You will drag individual blocks created below into this file, duplicate, rotate, and fine tune them.

Display a grid in this file to help lining up the blocks: select [Edit>Preferences>Grid] gridlines every 4", 2 subdivisions. Turn [View>Grid] on, Snap to grid on. Select [Window>Images>Cascade].

2. Create the image background.
- Select [File>Open] to open the image you want to use as the quilt block image. Select a photo that has two colors and an implied line separating the colors. The line can be diagonal like the image for this project, horizontal like the horizon, or vertical.
- Optional: Touch up the image if it needs it.
- Select the Square cookie cutter, set to Defined Proportions and Crop off. Drag the image around using Free Rotate until the intersection of the two colors is on the diagonal like the red line shown. The square can be crooked. Press <ENTER> to cut the cookie.
- Select [Image>Rotate>Straighten image].
- Rename the layer Photo.

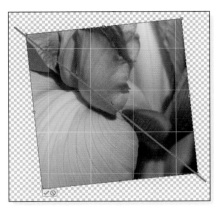

Implied diagonal superimposed on the image

- Select the Crop tool. On the Crop Options bar, set the image width and height to 8", 240 ppi resolution. Drag the mouse around the square, then press <ENTER>.
- Select [File>Save As] or press<CTRL SHIFT s> to save as filename.psd.

3. Prepare to create the four quilt blocks.

In steps 4–9 you will make each completed block in the quilt block file and then drag it to the design wall file. Each block uses parts from the previous block.

When you cut the cookies for the blocks, turn Crop off. Set shape options to Fixed Size: 8" wide, 8" high; from Center click to turn on. Make sure the cookie is centered on the grid before you press <ENTER>.

4. Create the Wave Filter layer.
- In the image quilt block file, duplicate the Photo layer twice <CTRL j>.
- On the top layer, from the top pull-down menu, select [Filter>Distort>Wave]. The example shows the Wave-square filter. Play with the filter — the result should show the implied diagonal line. Type OK. Merge down with the top Photo layer to remove any transparent parts of the Wave filter <CTRL e>.
- Rename this layer Wave by double clicking on its name in the Layers palette.
- Duplicate the Wave layer <CTRL j>. Click on the bottom Wave layer and hide it by clicking on its eye in the Layers palette.
- Click on the top Wave layer.

After applying and duplicating the Wave filter

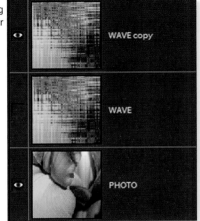

WAVE copy

WAVE

PHOTO

5. Quilt Block 1
- Select the Tile 3 Cookie Cutter and cut a shape from the top Wave layer. You will get an "X" composed of irregular dots cut from your filtered fabric. Rename this Layer Tile 3 (Dots).
- Select [Image>Rotate>Layer 180°].
- Apply layer styles such as Bevel and Drop Shadow. If it doesn't stand out enough from the background, darken it using [Enhance>Adjust Color>Color Variations].
- Unhide the bottom wave layer.

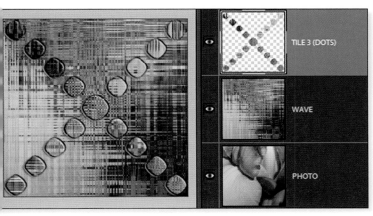

Block 1 showing layers

6. Save the block and move it to the design wall file.
- Save the block as a JPEG file to flatten the block, [File>Save As>filename.jpg] or PSD [File>Save>filename.psd] if you want to retain the layers.
- If you want to skip viewing and combining blocks in the design wall file, return to the image file now.
- To add the block to the design wall file, press <CTRL a> to select all, then select [Edit>Copy Merged] or press <SHIFT CTRL c>.
- Click on the design wall file. Select [Edit>Paste] or press <CTRL v>. Refer to the table in step 10 on page 77 for block positioning.
- Rename the layer with the quilt block number. For example, Block 1.
- You will duplicate and position the blocks in step 10 after you create them all.
- Return to the image block file.

7. Quilt Block 2 (Diamonds and Lines)
- Delete Tile 3 if it is still the top layer. You should have two layers: the Photo on the bottom and one Wave layer above it.
- Duplicate the Wave layer <CTRL j> and hide the bottom Wave layer by clicking on its eye.

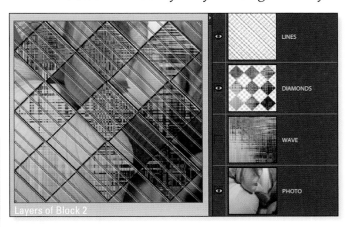

Layers of Block 2

a. Create the Diamonds layer:
- Select the Cookie Cutter, choose Tile 4, and set shape options to fixed size 8" x 8". Cut 9 diamonds at once with this Cookie Cutter from the top layer (Wave).
- Rename the layer Diamonds.
- Frost the edges, adding layer styles such as Bevels and Shadow so it will stand out from the Photo Layer.

b. Create the Lines layer:
- Create a new layer above the Diamonds layer <CTRL SHIFT n>, click on the Paint Bucket <k> and color it with the foreground color. Select the Cookie Cutter again, choose Tile 2. As you cut the diagonal lines from the solid-color layer, be sure they will be oriented along the same diagonal as the original image — free rotate the Cookie Cutter or type 90° in the Free Transform options bar before you cut it.
- Rename the new layer Lines.

c. Create the Shape outline:
- Select the Magic Wand <w>.
- Set the tolerance to 255 and turn Contiguous off on the options bar.
- Click on one of the stripes in the Lines layer stripe. This should cause all of the stripes to be highlighted.
- Press the Delete key. DO NOT TOUCH THE HIGHLIGHTED LINES YET!

○ Use "Stroke" to outline the areas that used to be filled with diagonal lines by selecting [Edit>Stroke Outline Selection]: Set the width to 20 px, and location to Inside. Stroke will use the current Foreground color unless you change it. Click on the color box. Move the mouse onto the image and select the color from your image that you want to use with the Eyedropper. Click OK. Press Esc to remove the highlighting.

- Repeat step 6 to move block 2 (the top left block) to the design wall file.

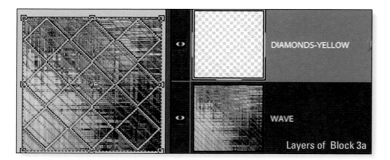

Layers of Block 3a

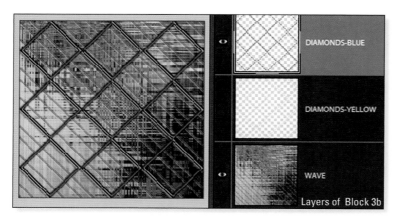

Layers of Block 3b

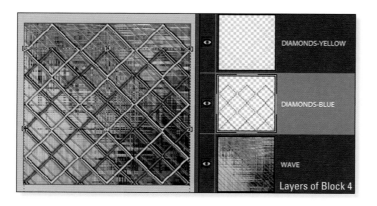

Layers of Block 4

8. **Quilt Block 3 (outline block 2 diamonds)**
Note: Make Block 2 before making Block 3.
a. Create Block 3a:
   ○ Unhide the Waves layer.
   ○ Hide the Diamonds layer, then merge the Lines, Wave, and Photo layers [Layer>Merge Visible] or press <CTRL SHIFT e>. You should have two layers: Diamonds and Wave.
   ○ Unhide and Click on the Diamonds layer.
   ○ As in 7c, use [Edit>Stroke] to outline the diamonds in the Diamonds layer following the directions described previously for Lines. The project example uses yellow lines.
   ○ Rename the layer Diamonds – your color.
   ○ We named it Diamonds – Yellow.
   ○ Apply layer styles such as Bevel or Drop Shadow to emphasize the results.
   ○ Repeat step 6 to move Block 3a to the design wall file.
b. Create Block 3b, changing the diamonds outline color:
   ○ Duplicate the outlined Diamonds layer <CTRL j>.
   ○ Make one of the copies invisible.
   ○ Click on the Paint Bucket tool, then hold down <alt> and click on a color in your image to change the foreground color.
   ○ Click on one of the lines in the diamond to change its color (blue in the example).
   ○ Repeat step 6 to move block 3b to the design wall file.

9. **Quilt Block 4 (show 2 diamonds outlines)**
   - Make quilt Blocks 2 and 3 before making Block 4.
   - Unhide Diamond layers. Drag one of the Diamond layers below the other, centering it and lining up the diamond tips at the bottom. The example shows the blue layer moved down and dragged below the yellow diamonds layer.
   - Repeat step 6 to move block 4 to the design wall file.
   - Save the block file [File>Save>filename.psd].

10. **Duplicate and position blocks on the design wall.**
In the design wall file, create duplicate quilt blocks and position them in the design wall file as shown in the table on page 77.

Table: Block Layouts on the Design Wall

Row	Column 1	Column 2	Column 3
1	Block 2	Block 4 rotate layer 90° left	Block 3a
2	Block 4 rotate layer 90° right	Block 2 rotate layer 180°	Block 1 rotate layer 90° right
3	Block 1 rotate layer 90° left	Block 3b	Block 2 rotate layer 90° left
4	Block 3a rotate layer 180°	Block 1 rotate layer 90° right	Block 4 rotate layer 90° right

Alternatively, play around with the blocks you have made and create your own layout. Select [Enhance>Adjust Color>Color Variations or Hue/Saturation]. For example, using Hue/Saturation, the yellow in rows 1 and 2, columns 2 and 3 blocks, was changed to yellow-green and lightened. Using Color Variations, the blocks in rows 3 and 4 were darkened slightly and the blocks in row 1 were lightened.

11. Finish the quilt.

Follow steps 5 through 8 in the Digital Design Wall section to add an optional digital border and print on fabric. The border in CHECKERBOARD was created with a blue background with a diagonal stripe pattern over it.

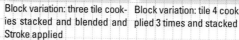
Variations on a Theme

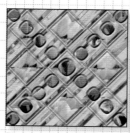
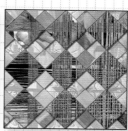
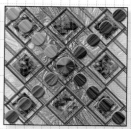

Block variation: three tile cookies stacked and blended and Stroke applied

Block variation: tile 4 cookie applied 3 times and stacked

Block variation: three tile cookies stacked and blended and Stroke applied

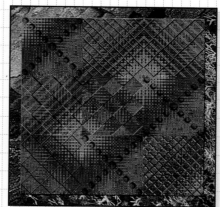
MOSSY REDWOODS digital quilt by Sandy Hart, 2008

Left, Digital quilt by Debbie Biller

Below, Digital quilt by Gudny Campbell. The Glowing Edges filter was applied to a quilt with an image of a pink flower and green leaves.

Right, Digital quilt by Gudny Campbell. Variation repeating one block, and playing with stroke and color.

PROJECT 7: OCEAN ROAD

Use a Digital Design Wall to create a quilt with multiple shapes cut with different cookie cutters arranged on a background composed of multiple blocks. The example we created for this project used just one scenic picture as it was taken and modified by a variety of Photoshop Elements filters. The Variations on a Theme suggests other possibilities using multiple pictures, backgrounds, and cookies.

Cookie shapes: (a) Circle Frame; (b) Whole Note; (c) River 1; and (d) River 2

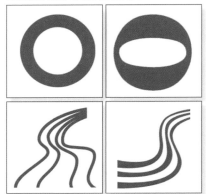

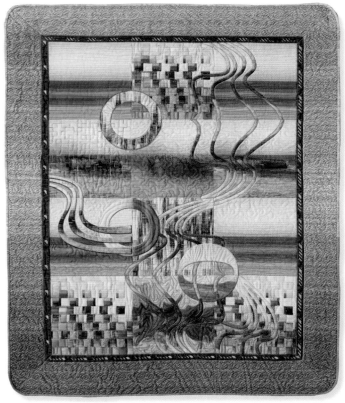

OCEAN ROAD, 32" x 40", by Gudny Campbell, 2008. Free-motion quilted, using the image shapes as guidelines following the horizontal ocean and ribbon lines.

Quilt Recipe

Cookie cutters:
  Circle Frame (in the Shapes submenu)
  Whole Note (in the Music submenu)
  River 1 and River 2 (in the Nature submenu)
Finished size: 24" x 32" without the optional border
  28" x 36" with the 2" border
Border: Four 2½" x 44" strips of a coordinating fabric
Backing and binding: 1 yard of a coordinating fabric
Batting: Crib-quilt-size piece
  (34" x 42" if a border is added)
12 sheets of 8½" x 11" treated, paper-backed fabric

Need to Know

- [Chapter 2 | THE BASICS]
- [Chapter 3 | DIGITAL STASH & COLOR PLAY]

New Skills
- Combining a photo with filters that reflect the photo
- Stacking shapes to create effects

Instructions:

1. **Open the design wall file and set preferences.**
   - Follow step 1 in the Digital Design Wall section to create the design wall file, setting the resolution to 240 ppi with a transparent background. Project file size is 24"x 32".

- Change the size as desired. Bookmark the Design Wall section page of this book as you will return to it later.
- Display a grid in this file to help lining up the blocks: select [Edit>Preferences>Grid] gridlines every 4", 2 subdivisions. Turn [View>Grid] on, [Snap To Grid] on. Select [Window>Images>Cascade].

2. Create the background photo block.
- Select an interesting photo with some contrast — it could be a scenic landscape or a close-up of a flower.
- Select [File>Open] or <o>.
- Click on the Crop tool or press <c>.
- Crop to 8" x 8", 240 ppi resolution.
- Save it as block.psd so you don't accidentally save the original image later.
- Apply Quick Fix if it needs it.
- Drag the image to the design wall file.

3. Create filtered quilt blocks.
- Click on the open block and duplicate the layer several times [CTRL j].
- Apply one or more filters on each layer.

  The following table shows the filters used. All of the filters may be found in the Layers palette on the right side of the workspace or in the pull-down Filters menu on top. Refer to Chapter 3: Digital Stash for more detail. The bottom layer shows the photo.

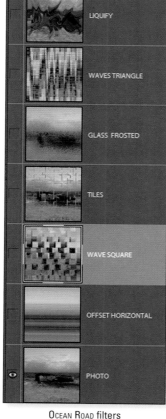

OCEAN ROAD filters

Some of the filters should reflect the original photo (for example, Offest and Liquify show the horizontal lines and the photo shows through Glass and Tiles).

- Drag each one to the design wall file and begin to arrange them. With the Block file and Digital Design Wall files open on the desktop, click on a filtered image (or its name in the Layers palette) and drag it into the Design Wall file. When you release the mouse button a copy of that image will be added to the destination file in a new layer. Continue making Filter layers until you have filled the background file.

- If you have already created a Digital Stash you want to use, open the files, crop them to 8" x 8", 240 ppi resolution, and drag them to the design wall file, instead of creating new filtered images in one PSD file. For example, Sandy could have used some of the images in her COASTAL PATH stash.

4. Arrange blocks in the design wall file.
Move <v> the blocks around until you are pleased with the background design. In Variations on a Theme, some of the quilt blocks were flipped to create a more flowing design. The background blocks used in the OCEAN ROADS quilt contain the filters listed in the table below. You may want to use the same filters, or different ones depending on the photo you start with and the effect you are trying to achieve.

OCEAN ROAD background

Table: Block Layouts on the Design Wall

Filter>Other>Offset Horizontal	Filter>Distort>Wave Square	Filter>Other>Offset Horizontal
Filter>Stylize>Tiles	Filter>Distort>Ocean Ripple	Original Photo
Filter>Other>Offset Horizontal	Filter>Distort>Wave Triangle	Filter>Other>Offset Horizontal
Filter>Distort>Wave Square	Filter> Distort>Liquify	Filter>Distort>Wave Square

5. **Align the quilt blocks and save.**
   - Select [View>Print Size]. Look at the spaces between the layers. Set grid on, then move the layers until they line up perfectly. To make very tiny adjustment right/left or up/down use the arrows keys.
   - Save the workspace file as a PSD with all the separate layers in case you want to change the background.
   - Select [VIEW>Fit on Screen]. You could stop here, and print the blocks without the cookie shapes on top (skip to step 8).

6. **Create the quilt file with one background layer.**
   - This step makes it easier to position cookies on a single background layer and reduces the file size. [Select>All] or <CTRL a>, then select [Edit>Copy Merged].
   - Then, create a new file [File>New>Image from Clipboard] <CTRL n>. Save it with a distinctive name (we will refer to it as the Quilt File).
   - Close the design wall file.

7. **Add cookies to the background.**
   Cookie shapes can add interest to a background, or hide flaws or digital block lines. The O̲c̲e̲a̲n̲ R̲o̲a̲d̲ appliqués added on top of the background were cut from the same original picture using the following cookie cutters: Circle frame, Whole Note, River 1, and River 2. Be creative and select cookies that fit your photo. Several of the quilts in Variations on a Theme use different cookies. Try creating a cookie outline as described in Project 5: B̲u̲b̲b̲l̲e̲s̲, Block 3. Try a Frosted Stack (duplicate a layer, cut a shape from the top layer, then add a Bevel, Glow, or Shadow). Refer to the Frosting section for details and examples.
   a. Create the cookie shapes: Return to the quilt block file and select one of the filtered layers or create a new one.
   - Duplicate it. <CTRL j>.
   - Cut a cookie shape from that layer. For the Circle Frame and Whole Note cookies, select Fixed Size = 6" x 6"; for the others select Defined Proportions.
   - Drag the result to the quilt file, and rename the layer to reflect the cookie shape.
   - Select other filter layers from the block file and repeat the process with the Circle Frame

cookie cutter again or with one or more of the other cookie cutters (e.g., Whole Note, River 1 or River 2).

b. Add layer styles to the cookies: O̲c̲e̲a̲n̲ R̲o̲a̲d̲ uses several layer styles on each appliqué to create the impression of depth. After you switch back to the quilt file, try different combinations of Shadows, Bevels, and Outer Glows and choose the effects that enhance each of your appliqués. Remember to double click on a style in Photoshop Elements 5, 6, or 7.

c. Duplicate and position cookies: Create an arrangement of appliqués like the O̲c̲e̲a̲n̲ R̲o̲a̲d̲s̲ quilt. Line them up like the picture, or play around with your own appliqués and come up with your own layout.
   - Create the O̲c̲e̲a̲n̲ R̲o̲a̲d̲s̲ layout. Select the move tool <v>. Resize the River 1 cookie so it is slightly wider than a background block and the same height by selecting its layer, clicking on the boundary box, and dragging it.
   - Duplicate the resized River 1 appliqué four times <CTRL j>, and position each one in the general area where it will end up. Zoom in and nudge the edges of the River 1 appliqués so they touch each other and line up.

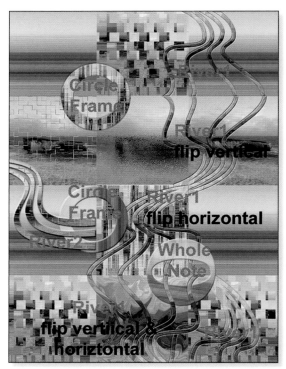

Positioning cookies on background

Resize the River 2 appliqué and position it on the left two blocks in the second and third rows, so it starts near the second row bottom left and ends near the third row bottom right.

d. Layer stacking order: Play with the shape layers stacking order and move layers up or down to create some really interesting effects. In Project 1 Variations on a Theme, STACKED HULAS, merged block column layers were moved up and down to give the effect of stacked columns.

To create the effect that some cookie shapes are stacked on top of or between others, follow the Layers palette stacking order as shown: In row 3, move the Circle Frame layer so it is on top of the River 1 layer and behind the River 2 layer.

Move the Whole Note layer so it is on top of the third row River 1 layer and behind the fourth row River 1 layer.

Save the file as [File>Save> quiltname.psd].

8. **Finishing**

Follow steps 5 through 8 in the Digital Design Wall section to add an optional digital border and print on fabric. The border in OCEAN ROADS was created with [Layer Styles>Pattern>Blanket and Bumpy] and then [Layer Styles>Photographic Effects>Teal Tone].

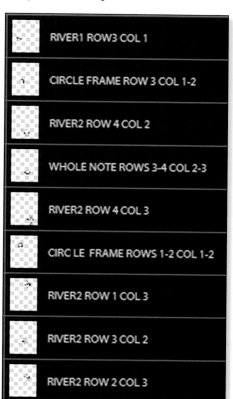

RIVER1 ROW3 COL 1

CIRCLE FRAME ROW 3 COL 1-2

RIVER2 ROW 4 COL 2

WHOLE NOTE ROWS 3-4 COL 2-3

RIVER2 ROW 4 COL 3

CIRC LE FRAME ROWS 1-2 COL 1-2

RIVER2 ROW 1 COL 3

RIVER2 ROW 3 COL 2

RIVER2 ROW 2 COL 3

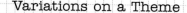

Variations on a Theme

Digital quilt by Debbie Biller

VICTORIA PARK, 30" x 36". Created and owned by Sandra Hart, 2008. Based on a photo of Victoria Park in Montreal with added frosted cookies on top that blend with the filtered photo.

Cookie layers stacking order

Digital quilt by Gudny Campbell of a poppy photo. Some of the blocks were rotated and flipped.

PROJECT 8: AUTUMN LEAVES

This table topper would be a perfect decoration for a fall table. Using the same technique, but different Cookie Cutters, a collection of table toppers could be made for different holidays or seasons: hearts for Valentines Day, shamrocks for St Patrick's Day, snowflakes for winter made with a Digital Stash or unfiltered close-ups of interesting textures. (see Variations on a Theme). Each block in the table-topper is composed of four orientations of a leaf cut from a half-square triangle block. Sandy chose two complementary designs from an autumn-hued Digital Stash for each block. For a larger wallhanging, simply increase block size, print more copies, or add two extra half-blocks and four 4" right triangles to extend the ends.

AUTUMN LEAVES table runner, 16" x 32". Created and owned by Sandra Hart in 2008. Printed on linen from Color Plus on an HP Designjet z3100 printer.

Quilt Recipe

6 Leaf Cookie Cutters: Foliage & Trees>
    Leaf 2, Leaf 4, Leaf 5, Leaf 6, Leaf 7, Leaf 16
Finished size: 16" x 32"
Backing and binding: 1 yard of a coordinating commercial fabric. An additional border could be added.
Batting: 20" x 36" piece (but this table topper is so small you can probably use scraps from other projects)
8 sheets of 8½" x 11" treated, paper-backed fabric

Leaf Cookie Cutters used

Need to Know

- Opening and saving files, creating a new layer [Chapter 2 | THE BASICS]
- Applying layer styles [Chapter 3 | FROSTING]
- Merging layers [Chapter 2 | MORE ABOUT LAYERS]
- Rotating a cookie layer [Chapter 2 | RESIZE, ROTATE & FLIP]

New Skills

- Cutting an image in half diagonally using only half of a cookie cutter

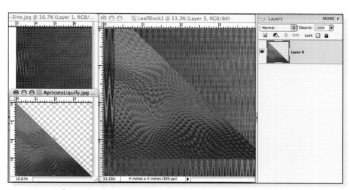

Dragging the 4" square and triangle into the Block file

> **Hint**
>
> Be sure to select the Move tool before moving layers from one file to another; if you forget and leave the Cookie Cutter tool selected, you may cut a cookie when you click on the work-space. If this happens, just type <CTRL z> or [Edit>undo].

Get ready:

1. **Open a new block file:** 4" x 4", 240 ppi, RGB file with a white background [File>New>Blank File] or <Ctrl n>.

2. **Open two Digital Stash files** that complement each other and arrange the three work areas on the desktop so all are visible.

Create a background for the appliqué:

1. **Crop one Digital Stash file** to a 4" x 4", 240 ppi square entering a "custom" size in the Crop Options menu above the workspace.

2. **Click on the second Digital Stash image and crop** it to 4" x 4", 240 ppi as well. Be sure that you can clearly see the edges of this file by zooming out <CTRL -> or increasing the window size of this file.

3. **Select the Cookie Cutter tool** <q> and the following options:
   Shape = Triangle
   Shape Options =
   Fixed size,
   8" wide x 4" high
   Feather = 0,
   Crop = off

4. **When the cookie cutter appears,** slide it to the left until only half of the cookie cutter is visible, creating a 4" half-square triangle. Press <ENTER> or [✓].

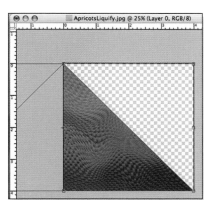

Cut a half-square triangle using just half of the original Cookie Cutter tool.

Create the appliqué:

1. **Select the Move tool** <v>. Click on the Digital Stash files and drag first the cropped square and then the triangle into the Block file. Close the stash files without saving. With both files open and visible on the desktop, click on the name of the layer to be moved and drag it to the destination file until the mouse pointer is centered. Then release the mouse button and a copy of the file will be created on a new layer. Select [File>Close] or press <CTRL w>.

2. **In the Block file, be sure the triangle is the topmost layer.** Drag the triangle so it neatly covers half of the square.

3. **Select both square and triangle layers** (by clicking on their labels with the shift key held down) and merge them [Layer>Merge Layers] or <CTRL e>. You have just learned how to make a half-square triangle block, the basis for hundreds of traditional quilt blocks!

4. **Duplicate this layer; press** <CTRL j>

5. **Rotate the top layer 180°** [Image>Rotate>Layer 180°]

6. **Select the Cookie Cutter tool** <q>:
   Shape = One of the leaf cookie cutters
   Shape Options = Defined Proportions
   Feather = 0, **Crop** = off

7. **Before cutting the leaf shape from the top layer,** free rotate the cookie cutter so it lines up nicely along the diagonal and fills most of the 4" half-square block. Press <ENTER> or [✓].

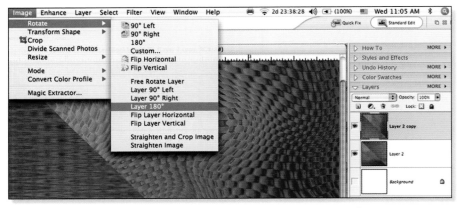

After merging and duplicating the square and triangle, rotate one copy 180°.

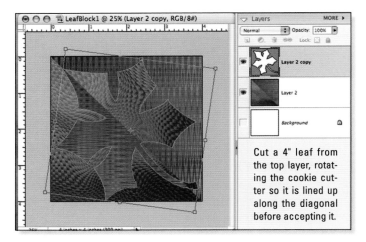

Cut a 4" leaf from the top layer, rotating the cookie cutter so it is lined up along the diagonal before accepting it.

3. **Duplicate the split-leaf block** three times; press <CTRL j>.

4. **Starting with the top layer,** move <v> one to each of the four corners, as described in Create the Appliqué on page 83, and arrange them so the leaves circle around the center with the stems touching as shown. [Image>Rotate>Rotate Layer Left, Right or 180]. Nudge the blocks until they just touch.

5. **Save the new 8" block** as a PSD if you think you might want to make changes or as a JPEG file which flattens it. [File>Save As] or press <CTRL SHIFT s>.

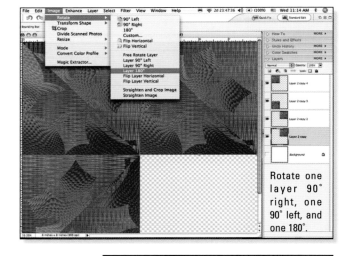

Rotate one layer 90° right, one 90° left, and one 180°.

A bevel was added to the leaves in this version.

Special effects:

Add a bevel, shadow, or some other layer style to the leaf shape that you just cut. [e.g., Styles & Effects>Layer Styles>Bevels>Simple Sharp] before you merge the leaf and background layers.

Create and arrange four versions of the block:

1. **Increase canvas size** to 8" x 8" <CTRL ALT c>.

2. **Select the leaf and background layers** by clicking on their labels with the shift key held down. Merge them by selecting [Layer>Merge Down] or pressing <CTRL e>.

Printing and finishing:

1. **Repeat the previous steps** to create 7 more sets of four split leaves, using a different leaf cookie cutter and different pieces of your Digital Stash for each one.

2. **To make the quilt as shown,** print the 8 split-leaf files.

3. After treating the printed blocks as recommended by the manufacturer, **trim** them to 8½" x 8½".

4. **Arrange your Split Leaf blocks** on a design wall until you are happy with the layout. Cut one in half, add triangles to each side as shown, then sew the blocks together. Add a border, if desired.

5. **Create a quilt sandwich** and quilt this table topper by outlining the leaves, adding veins and texture inside each leaf, and swirly textures in the background.

6. **Bind** as usual.

Variations on a Theme

You can achieve a completely different look by adding a Glowing Edges filter to the finished set of four blocks. Find this filter in the Stylize submenu of the Filter Gallery. It picks up textures in the Digital Stash and the edges of the bevel and turns them into neon outlines on a black background.

It is also possible to use different cookie cutters to create other seasonal quilt blocks that can be used for additional table toppers, pillow covers, place mats, or quilts. The next example shows a series of alternating pink and red heart shapes, cut in half vertically, recombined, and duplicated.

Finally, a more interesting version of the Leaf Ornament 1 block (see project 1) was created by cutting a 6" appliqué from one of two 8" half-square triangles. The resulting blocks were placed side by side creating an attic-windows-type sash around each block.

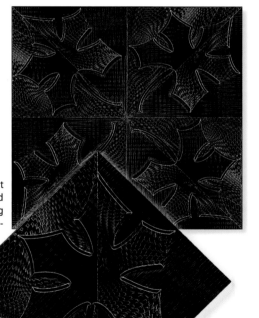

A completely different look was achieved by adding a Glowing Edges filter to the finished block.

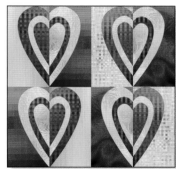

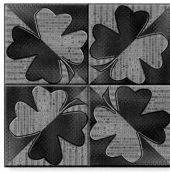

Examples of other seasonal images: split hearts, snowflakes, and shamrocks

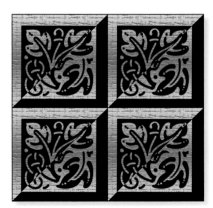

A new twist on Project 1, MOONLIT LEAVES

PROJECT 9: CALIFORNIA BEAUTY

CALIFORNIA BEAUTY is a new twist on an old favorite: New York Beauty. In our version, you create arcs, spikes, and other shapes with the Cookie Cutter tool and piece them digitally. Because there are so many different blocks in this quilt, the instructions will focus on general principles about how to construct CALIFORNIA BEAUTY blocks, rather than step-by-step instructions for each one. We will give exact dimensions for a few blocks to get you started, but encourage you to just play around; cut shapes then vary their size, order, color, and frosting to create your own designs. Finally, mix and match elements to create new designs.

CALIFORNIA BEAUTY, 32" x 40". Made and owned by Sandra Hart, 2007. It was printed on cotton poplin from Color Plus on an HP Designjet z3100 printer.

Cookie cutter shapes used to make CALIFORNIA BEAUTY blocks

Quilt Recipe

Cookie cutters: Quarter Circle; Triangle; Flower 22, 23, 24, 25, 28, and 29; Floral Ornament 2; Frame 34; Registration Target 2; Seal

Finished size: 32" x 40"

Backing and binding: 1½ yards of coordinating fabric

Batting: crib-quilt-sized piece at least 36" x 44"

20 sheets of 8½" x 11" treated, paper-backed fabric

Note: Blocks in the original quilt were 4½" square, however project quilt instructions are for 4" blocks so 4 can be printed per sheet of fabric. If you would rather make 8" blocks, simply double the dimensions given, except degrees of rotation.)

Need to Know

- Creating a Digital Stash [Chapter 3 | Creating & Embellishing "Fabric"]
- Cutting shapes with the Cookie Cutter tool [Chapter 2 | The Basics]
- Changing the size of shapes with Free Transform [Chapter 2 | Resize, Rotate & Flip]
- Applying Layer Styles [Chapter 3 | Frosting]

New Skills

- Cutting one quarter of Cookie Cutter shapes
- Shading or recoloring half of a shape
- Recycling elements of blocks

What to do:

New York Beauty blocks consist of plain or pieced centers, one or more pieced arcs, and a background. California Beauty blocks have a similar look, but are made with quarter circles, triangles, and wedges cut from circular shapes with interesting edges. The blocks are created with the center in the upper left-hand corner for simplicity. However, finished blocks are easy to rotate before you print or sew them together.

The examples were cut from painted layers for easy reference, but the instructions assume you will cut your pieces from photos or your Digital Stash. Experiment with frosting to add definition to the edges and dimensional effects. Pay attention to the appearance of the components and their order in the Layers palette; upper layers either hide or reveal lower layers to achieve the look of solid and pieced arcs from stacks of quarter circles and other shapes. We will be moving a lot of shapes from one file to another, so be sure your workspace is in Tile or Cascade mode and the files you are using are open, visible, and arranged in a logical way.

Hint

If the shapes that come with Photoshop Elements aren't enough, thousands more are available online for a minimal price. Sandy purchased one such shape and used it as an overlay for a few arcs in CALIFORNIA BEAUTY.

Get ready:

First, you will need to create a Digital Stash; Sandy used more than 100 photos of leaves and flowers, but here are some other ideas:

- Crayon colors for some of the blocks, black and white for others (turn any image black and white with [Enhance>Adjust Color>Remove Color]
- Muted creams, blues, and beiges to evoke a beach scene
- Fall leaves set off sky blue or bark brown
- Spring-like pastels with off-white
- Mix of close-up photos and Digital Stash

Use Hue/Saturation to create several versions of particularly nice textures in different colors to increase your stash. Or, if you don't want to build a Digital Stash, create the entire quilt using painted layers (see Variations on a Theme for an example).

Hint

Before you cut any pieces, check that the resolution of the Digital Stash file is the same as the Block file (I used 300 ppi) and at least 4" high and wide.

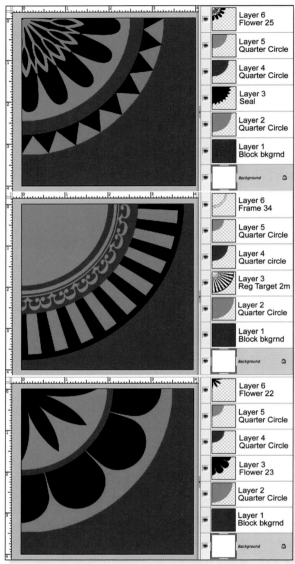

Easy California Beauty blocks: (a) Block 1, Tiny Spikes and Doily; (b) Block 2, Spokes and Lace; (c) Block 3, Floral

Start with a few simple blocks:

The following steps are for Block 1. Before using any image, be sure its resolution is 300 ppi and it is at least 4" x 4". Think about using an image more than once in this or other blocks.

1. **Create a Block file.**
   - Select [File>New>Blank File] or press <Ctrl n>, 4" x 4", 300 ppi, RGB, Background = white

2. **Cut a block background.**
   - Open a photo or Digital Stash file.
   - Use the Crop tool <c> option bar to cut a 4" x 4", 300 ppi square.
   - Drag it to the Block file <v>.

3. **Cut 3 quarter circles.**
   - Open 3 Digital Stash files.
   - Select the Cookie Cutter tool <q>.
   - **Shape** = Quarter Circle
   - **Shape Options** = Fixed size; refer to Table 1 for Block 1, Layers 2, 4, 5
   - **Feather** = 0 px; **Crop** = on
   - Move the Cookie Cutter over the best part of the image. Press <ENTER> or select [✓].
   - Drag each quarter circle into the Block file.

4. **Add a little easy "piecing."**
   In Block 1, Layer 3, the jagged edges of a "Seal" sandwiched between two quarter circles gives the look of pieced triangles.
   - Open a Digital Stash or photo file.
   - Select the Cookie Cutter tool <q>.
   - **Shape** = Seal
   - **Shape Options** = Fixed size **2 times** the width of the quarter circle it will cover
   - **Feather** = 0 px; **Crop** = on

		Layer 1	**Layer 2**	**Layer 3**	**Layer 4**	**Layer 5**	**Layer 6**
1		Square	Q Circle	Seal	Q Circle	Q Circle	Flwr 25
		4.0"	3.25"	6.5"	2.8"	2.5"	4.5"
				Cut ¼			Cut ¼
2		Square	Q Circle	RegTgt 2	Q Circle	Q Circle	Frame 34
		4.0"	3.75"	7.55"	2.75"	2.0"	5.2"
				Cut ¼			Cut ¼
3		Square	Q Circle	Flwr 23	Q Circle	Q Circle	Flwr 22
		4.0"	3.5"	6.5"	2.13"	2.0"	3.5"
				Cut ¼			Cut ¼

Table 1: Dimensions for Easy California Beauty Block Pieces

- To cut a perfect quarter wedge from any circular shape, slide the cookie cutter to the upper left-hand corner until its center symbol is on the edge. Press <ENTER> or select [✓] to cut it.
- Drag the cut shape into the Block file.

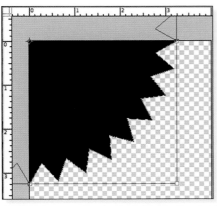 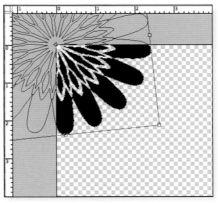

Cutting elements of a simple California Beauty block: (left) cutting a quarter of a circular shape to "piece" an arc; and (right) an appliqué for the center

---

Hint

The trick to cutting quarter-cookies is to zoom out on the file, <CTRL -> or use the zoom wheel if your mouse has one, grab the corner of the box around the workspace, and drag it until you can see gray background beyond the current workspace. If the image is smaller than the workspace, it will be surrounded by a light gray background, as shown.

---

5. **Decorate the center** (Block 1, Layer 6).
   - Open a Digital Stash file.
   - Select the Cookie Cutter tool <q>.
   - **Shape** = Flower 25
   - **Shape Options** = Fixed size **2 times** the width of the smallest quarter circle, the Center (Layer 5 in Figure 3a and Table 1)
   - **Feather** = 0 px; **Crop** = on
   - Slide the cookie cutter to the upper left-hand corner and position its center symbol on the edge of the file to cut a perfect quarter. Rotate the cookie cutter a little to center it. Press <ENTER> or select [✓] when satisfied.
   - Drag it into the Block file.

6. **Finish the block.**
   - Arrange the layers in the Block file in the order shown.
   - Save one version as a (flattened) JPEG file. <CTRL SHIFT s>

- Save the original as a PSD file so you can reuse some or all of the pieces in new blocks.
- Close all of the Digital Stash files without saving (<CTRL w>).

Congratulations! You now know all you need to know to create an easy California Beauty block. Try making the other 2 easy blocks, referring to page 88 and using the values in Table 1 to practice your skills. Then move on to the next type of block.

Create a block with triangle spikes:

Arcs filled with pieced spikes are characteristic of New York Beauty blocks. We make these with Cookie Cutter tools, but it takes a few steps: Cut the first spike with the Triangle Cookie Cutter tool, rotate it a prescribed amount, move it to the Block file, rotate it a little more, move it to the Block file again, and so on. When the correct number has been cut, arrange their tips around the outside of the larger quarter circle and the straight bases around the edge of the smaller quarter circle. The circumference of the smaller arc and the number of triangles you plan for that arc are used to calculate the width of the base of the triangles. But don't panic; we provide look-up tables to make cutting and rotating easy. We start with a simple block to demonstrate the steps.

1. **Create a background for the spikes.**
   - Open a blank, 4" x 4", 300 ppi file.
   - Color the background purple with the Paint Bucket <k>.
   - Create two new layers <CTRL SHIFT n> and use the Paint Bucket tool <k> to paint them blue and green as shown (see THE BASICS for more information).
   - With the Cookie Cutter tool, cut 3" x 3" and 2" x 2" quarter circles from Layer 2 (blue) and Layer 3 (green) respectively. TURN CROP OFF before this and the following steps.

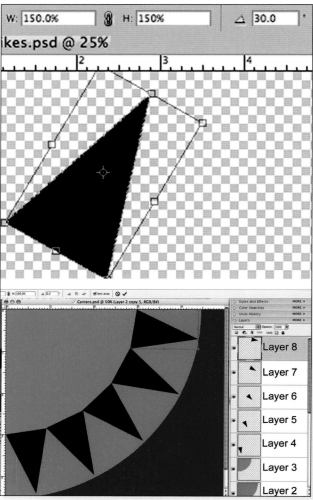

Rotating and positioning spikes on a quarter circle

2. Cut the spikes.
- Open a blank, 4" x 4", 300 ppi file.
- Paint it with the Paint Bucket <k>.
- Decide on the number of spikes you want (5 in the example).
- Select the Cookie Cutter tool <q>.
- **Shape:** Triangle
- **Shape Options:** Fixed size
  Width: Based on the width of the **smaller** of the quarter circles that will bracket the spikes; look it up in Table 2 (0.63" for 5 spikes around a 2" quarter circle).
  Height: Based on the visible "arc" the spikes will be placed on (the width of the larger Blue quarter circle minus the width of the smaller Green quarter circle): 1" in the sample
  Crop = OFF
- Cut the triangle.

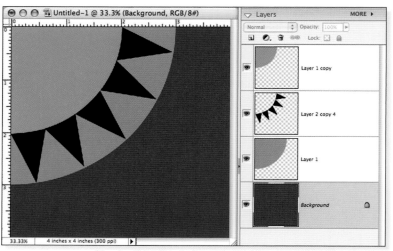

Merging the spikes and covering their bases

Width/height of quarter circle at base of Spikes (inches)									
Number of spikes	2.00	2.50	3.00	3.50	4.00	4.50	5.00	5.50	6.00
4	0.79	0.98	1.18	1.37	1.57	1.77	1.96	2.16	2.36
5	0.63	0.79	0.94	1.10	1.26	1.41	1.57	1.73	1.88
6	0.52	0.65	0.79	0.92	1.05	1.18	1.31	1.44	1.57
7	0.45	0.56	0.67	0.79	0.90	1.01	1.12	1.23	1.35
8	0.39	0.49	0.59	0.69	0.79	0.88	0.98	1.08	1.18
9	0.35	0.44	0.52	0.61	0.70	0.79	0.87	0.96	1.05
10	0.31	0.39	0.47	0.55	0.63	0.71	0.79	0.86	0.94

Table 2: Triangle Widths (based on the number of spikes you want on the arc and the circumference of the quarter circle that will cover its base. Formula: [(2 pi times width of Quarter Circle)/4]/number of spikes.

Hint

If the bases of the triangles don't quite touch (or the quarter circle doesn't cover them once you've added "frosting"), move the triangles a little closer to the upper left and/or slightly alter the width and height of the quarter circle.

3. **Rotate the spikes.**
   - Select Free Transform <CTRL t> or [Image>Transform> Free Transform]
   - In the rotate box of the Free Transform Options bar, enter the value from the row in Table 3 corresponding to the number of triangles to place on that arc. In the example, first rotate the triangle 99°. Then rotate it an additional 18° on each subsequent rotation.
   - After each rotation, drag the result into the Block file until the correct number of triangles are arranged around the edge of the quarter circle.

Amount to rotate each triangle (in degrees)										
Number of Spikes	1st	2nd	3rd	4th	5th	6th	7th	8th	9th	10th
4	101.3	22.5	22.5	22.5						
5	99.0	18.0	18.0	18.0	18.0					
6	97.5	15.0	15.0	15.0	15.0	15.0				
7	96.4	12.9	12.9	12.9	12.9	12.9	12.9			
8	95.6	11.3	11.3	11.3	11.3	11.3	11.3	11.3		
9	95.0	10.0	10.0	10.0	10.0	10.0	10.0	10.0	10.0	
10	94.5	9.0	9.0	9.0	9.0	9.0	9.0	9.0	9.0	9.0

Table 3: Degrees to Rotate Each Spike (based on the number of spikes)

4. **Arrange triangles.**
   As shown on page 90, arrange the 5 triangles around the lower arc.

5. **Select all of the triangles** (click on their names with the shift key held down) and merge them <CTRL e> or [Layer>Merge Down].

6. **Arrange layers.**
   If necessary, arrange layers in the order shown on page 90.

Split-half spikes

You may have noticed that some of the spikes in California Beauty appear to be pieced. To accomplish this quickly and easily, follow these steps before rotating and duplicating the triangles:
1. **Select** the rectangular Marquee Tool <m>.
2. **Drag** it over half of the triangle, using arrow keys to position it.
3. **Use** the Paint Bucket <k> or Hue/Saturation <CTRL u> to change the appearance of half of a painted triangle.
4. **Use** Hue/Saturation <CTRL u> or [Enhance>Adjust

A California Beauty block with split spikes

Color>Color Variations] if the triangle was cut from a photo or Digital Stash. Play around until you are happy with the result.

5. **Press** <esc> to remove the Marquee box. This would also be a good time to add a layer style, such as a bevel.

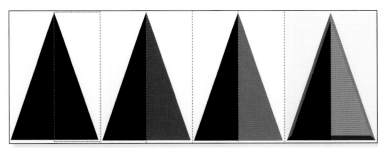

Enhancing a spike by making half of it brighter or a different color, or adding frosting

Use what you have learned

1. **Cut the following shapes** from your Digital Stash to create the block shown on page 92.
   Layer 1: 4" square
   Layer 2: 3¾" quarter circle. Frost it with a Simple Outer bevel.
   Layer 3: Quarter of a 7½" Flower 28. Frost it with a Low Drop Shadow.
   Layer 4: 3" quarter circle. Frost it with a Simple Outer bevel.
   Layer 5: Five spikes cut and rotated as described above
   Layer 6: 2" quarter circle with a Simple Outer Bevel
   Layer 7: Quarter of a 3½" Flower 24 frosted with a Simple Embossed Bevel and Low Drop Shadow

2. Finish the block.
- Arrange the layers in the Block file in the order shown.
- Save one version as a (flattened) JPEG file. <CTRL SHIFT s>
- Save the original as a PSD file so you can reuse some or all of the pieces in new blocks.
- Close all of the Digital Stash files without saving. <CTRL w>

Printing and finishing:

1. To make your CALIFORNIA BEAUTY, **arrange completed blocks in groups of four in a new file.** Consider rotating them as you arrange them so the final result is more interesting. To print 4 to a page:
   - Open a new 8" x 8", 300 ppi, RGB file. <CTRL n>
   - Open 4 Block files. Select [File>Open] or press <CTRL o>.
   - Drag each block into the blank file.
   - Arrange them so they just touch. If you have a layout in mind, be sure you want these blocks next to each other in the top square.
   - Print.

2. After treating the printed blocks as recommended by the manufacturer, **trim each group of four** to 8½" x 8½".

3. **Arrange groups of 4 blocks** before you sew them together to get the best effect.

4. **Add a border,** if desired.

5. **Create a quilt sandwich** as you would with any quilt; baste.

6. **Start by quilting in the ditch** to emphasize the shapes, and then free-motion quilt an interesting motif in the corner of each block.

7. **Bind** as usual.

WHEN I AM BREATHLESS, I WEAR PURPLE. Made and owned by Maris Azevedo, 2008. Printed on cotton broadcloth on an HP Designjet z3100.

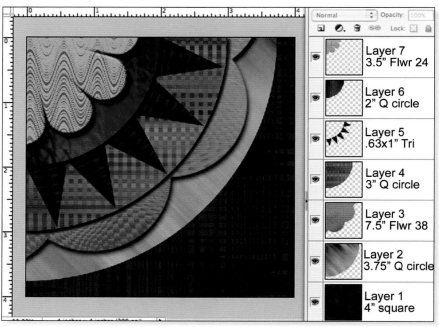

A frosted CALIFORNIA BEAUTY with spikes

| Layer 7 3.5" Flwr 24 |
| Layer 6 2" Q circle |
| Layer 5 .63x1" Tri |
| Layer 4 3" Q circle |
| Layer 3 7.5" Flwr 38 |
| Layer 2 3.75" Q circle |
| Layer 1 4" square |

New tricks

Maris Azevedo made the same blocks, but superimposed each block on a larger square of her Digital Stash, rotating them a bit left or right to add motion. She created the quilt in gratitude for the ten "extra" years of life given to her by the lifesaving stents depicted in the CT scan of her lungs. This image, shown in the lower right-hand corner of the quilt, was the basis of the Digital Stash she created to make the quilt.

Variations on a Theme

Gudny Campbell made her own version of the CALIFORNIA BEAUTY quilt but in a more freeform way than the original. Notice the way her spikes extend beyond arcs or are placed on top of the background itself. Rather than trying to imitate paper-pieced New York Beauty arcs, she simply created something beautiful with her own flower photos and Photoshop Elements Cookie Cutters. She also created a border with one filtered photo.

FLORAL BEAUTY, 24" x 32". Created and owned by Gudny Campbell, 2008. Printed on cotton broadcloth on an HP Deskjet z3100.

MIDNIGHT BEAUTIES, 15" x 37". Created and owned by Sandy Hart, 2008. Printed on cotton on an HP Designjet z3100.

You can enlarge an 8", 240 ppi square block to 12" at 160 ppi or reduce it with no visible loss of resolution. Far greater changes usually print just fine, as well. Have fun resizing and reusing your creations. A few suggestions in text and photo:

• Shrink a block way down and print many of them on a fabric sheet to produce Artist Trading Cards, or postcards to trade or give as gifts.

• Make a doll quilt for a child.

• Create coordinated place mats, coasters, and table runner.

• Print a block on artist's canvas (available in office supply stores) and hang with or without a frame.

• Print one or more blocks on photo paper, then mat and frame.

• Use one as a logo on your business cards.

• Print a Digital Stash creation or a block on silk and create tube beads.

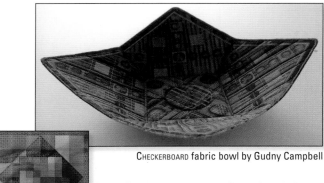

CHECKERBOARD fabric bowl by Gudny Campbell

SQUARE COOKIES block inchie by Gudny Campbell

COOKIE BEAUTY tote bag by Sandy Hart

COOKIE BEAUTY and SQUARE COOKIES eye glass cases by Sandy Hart

OCEAN ROAD quilt note card by Gudny Campbell

Card Back text

Card Back text

Page layout for two 4½" x 5½" portrait note cards

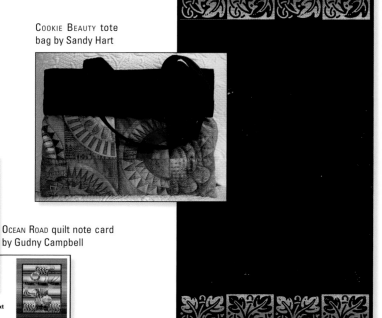

MOONLIT LEAVES table runner

The window effect was created by applying Layer Styles – Inner Shadows high to 16 beach photos for a scrapbook page by Sandy Hart.

RETINAL BEAUTY pillow by Sandy Hart

Frame from HULA quilt blocks

SOFTWARE, ETC.

Sources for
Adobe® Photoshop® Elements Software:
Most of the sources offer older versions as well as the latest versions at reduced prices. It is possible that an earlier version might be more compatible with your computer and operating system: http://www.adobe.com, http://www.amazon.com/

Graphic Xtras – Thousands of add-on shapes, brushes, gradients, patterns for Photoshop Elements, some free. This is where Sandy bought the additional Cookie Cutter by Abneil Software Ltd she used in the CALIFORNIA BEAUTY Project. http://www.graphicxtras.com/products/photoshopaddons.htm

SOFTWARE TIPS AND ADVICE

Adobe has a support Web site for Photoshop Elements with product help at http://www.adobe.com/support/photoshopelements/

Adobe Photoshop Elements Techniques newsletter has great tips and step-by-step articles. http://www.photoshopelementsuser.com

The Photoshop Elements 6 Book for Digital Photographers by Scott Kelby and Matt Kloskowski gives you tips and tricks for correcting, editing, sharpening, retouching, and presenting your photos like a pro. http://www.kelbytraining.com/?page=browse&category=photoshop-elements

About.com: Graphics Software offers tips, tutorials, and free downloads for Adobe Photoshop Elements. http://graphicssoft.about.com/od/pselements/Photoshop_Elements_Tutorials_and_User_Resources.htm

Epson Web site has all sorts of tips about printing and project ideas. http://www.epson.com/cgi-bin/Store/LearnCreate/

Hewlett Packard Web site has a wealth of information about printing on fabric, even though they don't sell any products specifically for that purpose (except, of course for copiers and printers). http://www.hp.com

FABRIC & RELATED SUPPLIES

BubbleJetSet 2000 Web site is http://www.prochemical.com.

Color Plus Fabrics – Many sizes and weights of paper-backed silk and cotton, rolls of paper-backed, pretreated fabric. They will also print your digital image on their fabrics using their wide-format printers. (612-382-0013) http://colorplusfabrics.com/

Dharma Trading Co. carries paper-backed cotton, silk, or organza; precut freezer paper for backing; Bubble Jet Set 2000; rolls of silk (cut to length for banners, scarves); transfer paper; and plain clothing onto which you can transfer images. Be careful about which silk product you order—some require steam to set the color permanently. They are helpful and informative. (800) 542-5227 http://www.dharmatrading.com/

Electric Quilt Printables – Another line of fabric sheets available in quilt stores and online. http://www.electricquilt.com.

Fibrecrafts carries treated, paper-backed organza, cotton, and silk. http://www.fibrecrafts.com/

Printed Treasures – Another brand of high-quality fabric sheets available in quilt stores and online. http://softexpressions.com/

Rupert, Gibbon & Spider offers many weights and sizes of treated, paper-backed fabric. http://www.silkconnection.com/

VV Graphics – Paperback books, treated fabric, photo CDs and instructional CDs. http://www.vvprints.com/

SOURCES FOR DIGITAL IMAGES

(There are thousands of others, but check their rules about downloading and using the images you find.)

http://science.nationalgeographic.com/science/photos
http://www.webshots.com/homepage.html
http://www.morguefile.com